MONASTERY OF THE VISITATION
5820 CITY LINE AVENUE
PHILADELPHIA 31, PENNSYLVANIA

Prophetic Intervention in the History of Man

alba house. DIVISION OF THE SOCIETY OF ST. PAUL
STATEN ISLAND, N.Y. 10314

Prophetic Intervention in the History of Man

Evode Beaucamp, O.F.M.

This book was originally published in French under the title *Le Prophétisme et l'Élection d'Israël* by Editions Fleurus, Paris.

Translated by Paul Garvin

Nihil Obstat
    Donald Panella, S.T.L., S.S.L.
    Censor Librorum

Imprimatur
    Joseph P. O'Brien, S.T.D.
    Vicar General, Archdiocese of New York
    May 7, 1970

Library of Congress Catalog Card Number 76-129176

SBN: 8189-0191-8

Designed, printed and bound in the U.S.A. by the Pauline Fathers and Brothers of the Society of St. Paul, 2187 Victory Blvd., Staten Island, N.Y. 10314 as part of their communications apostolate.

CONTENTS

INTRODUCTION

FUNDAMENTAL PRINCIPLES IN THE CHOICE OF ISRAEL AS GOD'S PEOPLE

The Bible is not a revelation about God, but God's Revelation. For thousands of years mankind tried to penetrate the deep silence surrounding the Godhead, but in spite of sacrifice and prayer it had been unable to emerge from the world in which it lived to establish a dialogue with the Lord of the Universe. With all the magical arts common to all religious systems and the temple oracles mankind heard only the echo of its own appeal, its own voice answering. This would have gone on indefinitely if outside history and time, a Voice had not made itself heard, saying: "It is I. *Here I am!*"

However sudden and unexpected it might seem, God's solemn entrance into history was nonetheless an answer to an appeal from mankind. It was the constant object of hope, awaiting and preparation. The God who spoke to Moses in the burning bush was the same God of the promise: "I am Yahveh, the God of your fathers"; and on becoming flesh the Word declared that he came "unto his own." Not less in the New Testament than the Old, the voice that says "Here I am" does not seem strange to the human ear. When the Most High speaks, it is as one who is "known."

In the meeting that takes place and in the dialogue that is opened and continues, it is God alone who takes the initiative and intervenes freely at the moment he decides and which no one could ever forecast. Before man has had the time to grasp the full sense of his presence, God has already vanished. It is impossible to become accustomed to him, because he never manifests himself in a complete or continuous manner. He approaches and then withdraws, that he may be sought with grief and in darkness. This alternation of appearance and absence, stressed in the Canticle of Canticles, was to become a fundamental law of Christian mysticism.

But the God of the Bible is not only the God who comes out from his silence in answer to mankind's cry. He is also an operating Will, and his action is the execution of a plan. He appears to Moses for the purpose of freeing the Hebrews from bondage in Egypt and making them a people. Yahveh was always to remain a God who sees and is unseen, who takes hold but is never possessed. He lays his hand on whom he wills, but no mortal hand can ever clasp it.

In the desert of Sinai Israel saw the skies rent and the mountains tremble on their foundations at Yahveh's voice, while the lightning flashed and hail decimated hostile armies. Before such a God Israel could measure her own powerlessness. He was not a God of storms whose secret powers could be tapped, as primitive peoples attempted to do when they fashioned images of their deities. Yahveh would not let himself be used as a tool. He would never reveal the secret of his power. "I am who am," he says of himself.[1]

---

1. Yahveh appears in this verse from Exodus (3, 14) to be unwilling to satisfy Moses' curiosity, asking him his name: "I am who I am, it is no concern of yours." In the ancient world to know a person's name, especially a god's, was to possess the secret of his power. Yahveh thus shows his intention of treating Israel as a Lord whose hand is not to be forced. But we should note that such a reply is not in accord with the words that follow: "This is what you shall say to the children of Israel: I AM has sent me to you." The short phrase seems to break the literary unity of the passage, so that some exegetes consider it a gloss. This seems probably. The divine name Yahveh means "He is" in the sense of "He is there," "It is

God exercises his control over a person withdrawing him from his surroundings. Abraham is ordered to leave the plain of Chaldea and journey towards the land of Promise. The Hebrews are ordered to leave the Nile valley for the land of Canaan. For neither could there be any question of ever returning to their point of departure. Before going to seek a wife for Isaac among his master's kinsfolk, Eliezer promises that, if his mission should fail, he will not take the young man back to the country of his fathers. On crossing the Red Sea the Hebrews close the way to an eventual return. In Deuteronomy it is recommended that the king shall not make his people return to Egypt to acquire horses, for Yahveh has said "you must never go back that way again" (Deut. 17, 16).

If God draws out, it is in order to draw to himself. Whomever God draws belongs afterwards only to him, he becomes his property, henceforth sacred, and nobody has a right to lay a hand on him. From the first, Yahveh declares himself to be a jealous God, not only in the sense that he will not tolerate the presence of any other divinity beside him but, in a deeper sense, that he intends to be the only ruler of his people. He alone will regulate the life of his elect, and outside of him there is to be no power, human or divine, that may influence the destiny of Israel in any manner whatsoever. To maintain his sovereign authority over the chosen people, his range of action, as the Bible shows us, goes on progressively increasing. When the kingdoms of Samaria and Jerusalem are drawn into the current of world history, it is Yahveh who is working behind all the great events on which the destiny of Israel depends. As the Lord of Israel he then shows himself as the Lord of the world.

He," a declaration of God's active presence at the center of events. Even if it is a gloss, however, it should not be neglected. It adds an important shade of meaning to the first sense of "He is," and is in harmony with the whole of biblical tradition. Yahveh is who He is — the unknowable, "apophatic" aspect of his action in history.

The corollary to this is the demand that Israel should belong exclusively to her God. She is expressly forbidden to take part in the political maneuvers of either the small neighboring countries or the great powers. Her role is to keep apart from any system of alliances, offensive or defensive. Since Yahveh takes upon himself, solely and completely, the defense of his people without anybody else's help, he is the only valid support to which Israel can look. The alternative to rejecting his guiding hand is ruin, bondage and death.

The laws of history that explain the rise and fall of civilizations do not apply to God's people. The life of Israel falls outside the immanent order of nature; her preservation and progress depend entirely on God's action, a design and a choice of God's, just as her decay and disappearance are the penalty for her resistance to God's will. Like an unstable body which can keep its balance by an acceleration of movement, so the chosen people would continue to exist as long as they accepted the movement given them by God's hand which in a mysterious manner tended to raise it above the world and above itself. Empires fall once they have no longer enough strength to resist pressure from outside; none of them can hope to last forever. The time of Israel's experience, on the contrary, is indefinite, or at least outside human calculation. Only an accident could bring it abruptly to an end, and the greater the height to which she had risen, the more resounding would her fall be. The conflict between life and death inherent in every living being is for Israel a constantly offered choice with a dramatic alternative: acceptance of God's wish to ascend without pause, or a headlong fall into the abyss.

Exempt from the laws of history, Israel is not amenable to the world's judgment. Her history cannot be explained from the outside. Her successes and failures are only understandable in the light of her behavior with reference to God's design, which the world does not see. Whom God has chosen is answerable to God alone, to him he is to express his gratitude and confess his sins. No other dialogue is possible except between God and his chosen one; whoever would come between them would be only an intruder. The mutual relationship must be enveloped in the privacy of love, the "royal secret" that was to be perfected in the silence of the Blessed Virgin—"And Mary kept all these things in her heart."

When Yahveh lays his hand upon the Hebrews, makes them his people, commands them to live apart under his protection, does it mean that Israel is to be a world closed in on itself, morally self-sufficient, with no ties of fellowship with the rest of the world? How could the chosen people consider the fact of their having been chosen without posing the problem of the rest of mankind? Obviously they had been preferred to all others, but would Yahveh remain a slave to his choice? Before his people existed, he is, and his choice could surely turn elsewhere. Hence the covenant of Sinai necessarily has a place in time and space. The Egyptians and Babylonians knew hardly anything outside their own history, but the story of Israel belongs from the very beginning to the development of world history and the general pattern of the destiny of mankind.

Her exceptional adventure could not remain without interest for the rest of the world. Though not entitled to judge her, the gentile nations have their eyes fixed upon her. She stands before them as a witness to what God can perform among men, and she bears the responsibility of her God's glory. Her disasters not only call forth the sarcasm of her neighbors but are damaging to the glory of Yahveh's name. Her successes would perhaps arouse, besides envy, respect among them for the name of Yahveh a first timid step towards the recognition of his authority. Were not all generations to be blessed by the name of Abraham? The experience of the chosen people, in short, is meant to be a pilot-experience, from which the world is invited to learn a lesson. Of this the Bible provides at least a confused notion.

Many commentators hold that after the Exile Jewish thought wavered between a narrow nationalism and a comparatively open universalism. These two tendencies, in fact, go well together.

They are not contradictory but complementary, and could in no case be analyzed separately. The Bible affirms at once both the unique and incommunicable character of Israel's experience and its witness value for the world.

When using the terms nationalism and universalism here, it must be borne in mind that the relation between the two ideas in Israel is an absolutely original one. It is a law of any live force that it tends to develop as widely as possible. Humanity is not exempt from this law; any spiritual or political force in the world always seeks to expand. What is different in the case of Israel is that, even though concerned about the salvation of the world, it never feels the temptation to leave its first homeland and overflow into other lands. It does not turn towards the outside world; it is the outside world which is attracted towards it.

This is understandable: how could Israel have ambitious aims towards her neighbors when God's gift was meant to satisfy her? She seeks only the free possession of her land, the heritage Yahveh has given her. Outside this sacred soil she feels at home nowhere.

It is true that the inspired writers, from Isaiah to the last of the apocalyptic prophets, never cease to invoke the triumph of the chosen people over the nations banded against them, but it must be noted that this drama is not enacted outside of Palestine, and that the final battle is fought around Jerusalem on the holy mountain. The foreign armies feel the weight of Yahveh's almighty power because they are trespassing on the soil of Israel. It is they who are the aggressors against a people who are quietly at home in their own country and have no need of the rest of the world.

But though Israel shows no sign of systematic aggressiveness towards other peoples, she is nevertheless the object of almost general hostility. The world will not admit an exception to its own way of life. It was just as difficult for the eighth century empires before Christ to tolerate the neutrality of Judah as for Hellenistic thought to accept the heterogeneity of Jewish culture.

Thus, through no fault of her own, Israel was to be attacked by other nations, but it was precisely this attack which by its failure was to give the world a chance of finding salvation and reveal Yahveh's glory to all.

The chosen one is snatched away from the world by God's hand; paradoxically, he is removed from the world only to be of better service to it. His very life itself is the most eloquent testimony.

❉ ❉ ❉

The choice of Israel is regulated by a series of laws which are strikingly coherent, but it would be useless to try to find a systematic account of them in the Bible. It was the mission of the prophets to draw them out gradually and make them evident throughout the years when historical events were deciding Israel's destiny. It was their task, as difficulties arose and increased, to propose a line of conduct which would allow the people of God to remain faithful to the Covenant in its main principles.

In this respect, however, the prophets were not innovating anything. The principles are the same as those that guided the people of Moses from the beginning, but they had been lived experimentally and concretely for a long time—it could hardly be otherwise—before being reflected upon. Israel needed to attain a certain degree of historical maturity and be capable of undertaking her responsibilities towards her God for this to be possible. From the desert to the end of the conquest of Canaan she had allowed herself to be moulded by God and had responded to his commands. Later on, after growing up, she would have to accept them freely. This was the time when the dialogue with Yahveh would begin in earnest, when she would become aware of what God expected from her and be strong enough to sustain the spiritual combat, finally meriting the name that summed up her whole destiny: "He who contends with God" (Gen. 32, 29).

The period when Israel reached adult status can probably be dated from the beginning of the monarchy. The final federation of the tribes, the unification of the national territory, the creation of a civil, religious and military administration, the establishment of a capital city, the construction of a national temple, all these are to be placed to the credit of David and his son. Henceforth the people of God was established on earth as a free and independent nation aware of itself.

The debate between God and his people could now begin. On one side it was carried on through the king and the country's leaders, on the other by the prophets as witnesses to the demands of the Covenant. The prophets are thus the true continuers of the work of Moses and the incarnation of his spirit. What distinguishes them from him, however, was that Moses was a leader invested with the power to assemble and guide the people, while the prophets can only express Yahveh's will without being able to impose it. Though they endeavor by their words to lead Israel back to Yahveh's rule, she has now become a nation and is autonomous in making her decisions.

The king for his part also claimed to speak in the name of Yahveh, especially when giving judgment. Both in Samaria and Jerusalem his kingly power was theocratic. In any case, before the rise of the Aryan empires, there was no state with a purely secular basis. With slight variations according to time and place, the king everywhere represented the national divinity as vicar and son. But the authority that the God of Sinai intended to exercise over his people was of quite a different order.

We must be careful not to mistake the real nature of the theocratic kingship of Israel. It could turn out in practice to be nothing but a convenient façade for withdrawing from Yahveh's rule. It is of little importance whether the different dynasties that succeeded each other in Samaria were Yahvehistic or not. Whatever the divine name invoked there, it was no longer Yahveh who actually ruled or took the initiative. This explains Yahveh's answer when Samuel consulted him after the Elders had gathered at Rama to ask for a king like other peoples:

"Hearken to the voice of the people all that they say to thee, for they have not rejected thee, but me that I should not reign over them." (1 Sam. 8, 7)

This answer may appear strange, for, according to the ceremonial in use in Oriental courts, it was usually on the occasion of the enthronement of a monarch that the kingship of the national god over the country was proclaimed. But everything depends, obviously, on what is meant by the kingship of God. The type of divine kingship proclaimed in the New Year rites was hardly compatible with the essential principles of the Covenant. The freedom of divine choice was entirely absent from them.

Assur and Marduk were acclaimed in Nineveh and Babylon and hailed as kings when they were considered as taking over the guidance of their country to assure its peace and prosperity. On each occasion there was a strengthening of the ties that united the god to his people and their land. But by his nature, Yahveh was not tied either to Israel or to Palestine. He had formed a people from serfs, and as a favor had given them a country belonging to other peoples and other gods. The settlings of Israel in Canaan was the result of an entirely free act on his part.

It should be added that the kingship of the national god was closely bound up with the cyclic round of the seasons, and the proclamation of it was renewed yearly in order to preserve all its effectiveness. Obviously Yahveh's transcendental action could not be tied down to the rhythm of nature. The benefits he bestows on his people proceed from his initiative alone. No one can force his hand or foretell the time or manner of his action.

The northern tribes, quicker to settle down than the southern ones, were also the first to adopt the ways of thought of the neighboring peoples in spite of their incompatibility with the spirit of the Covenant. It was among them, in fact, that the first experiments in kingship were tried in Israel with Gideon and his sons. They tended to make Yahveh a God resembling the gods of the peoples around them. He was represented, for instance, in the shape of a bull, the symbol of fertility and life; a goddess-spouse was found for him, and to comply with the diplomatic usages of the times, he was requested to show tolerance towards the gods introduced into Israel by foreign princesses.

In this and other ways the kingdom of Samaria turned completely aside from the Covenant. Elijah had to flee to Horeb to escape Jezebel's wrath and to hear again the forgotten voice of the God of Moses. With its nature thus changed, the monarchy could not but be condemned by whoever remained faithful to the reality of God's choice of Israel. No northern king could find favor in the eyes of the inspired writer of the Book of Kings. The efforts of the prophets to bring the erring people back under the hand of Yahveh were doomed to failure from the outset.

At Jerusalem, however, the monarchical principle seemed less questionable. While sparing none of the Samaritan rulers, the sacred writer does not fail to name the kings of Judah who walked in the ways of their father David. This criterion was decisive, for David had made it clear when he founded his dynasty that he intended to respect the ancient covenant. Profoundly religious, he had always been careful never to force the hand of Yahveh and to recognize the transcendence of his action. When, fleeing from Absalon, for example, the old king sees Sadoc the priest coming to meet him with the Ark, he exclaims:

Carry back the ark of God into the city. If I shall find grace in the sight of Yahveh, he will bring me again, and he will show me it and his tabernacle. But if he shall say to me: Thou pleasest me not; I am ready. Let him do that which is good before him. (2 Sam. 15, 25-26)

Yet the establishment of the Davidic monarchy was to have unfortunate results. It meant that Israel was now grown up and could choose for herself whether to accept or reject the authority of Yahveh. Choice means possibility of sin, and David himself affords a striking example. However great it may be, good will on the part of men has a limit; Israel would never succeed in conforming her conduct completely to the requirements of her God. An ever increasing gap is evident during the progress of the dialogue between Yahveh and his people, and between the prophets and the rulers of Juda. One day it was to become clear that the nation was fundamentally sinful. The human heart can belong fully to God only in the measure it allows itself to be fashioned by his hands. The emancipation of the chosen people and the free exercise of their liberty showed how impossible it was to respect the terms of the covenant when they came to rely on themselves, but at least the experience brought them to a knowledge of sin and of what grace would be.

The history of the prophetic office seems to be the story of a failure. For over three centuries the prophets fought might and main to bring the internal and external policies of the kingdoms of Samaria and Judah into line with their responsibilities as the chosen people. They did not succeed, but their mission bore fruit in another manner and in a wider field. By announcing the end of the Old Covenant, the last of the great prophets held out the hope of a New Covenant to be written in the hearts of the faithful. After this essential message, the prophetic office had no further purpose and could disappear.

There was nothing left but to await the coming of the Servant of Yahveh who would be the Prophet *par excellence* and who would fully satisfy the requirements of God's choice, the founder of a new people in whom the human and divine will would be completely identified: " My food is to do the will of him who sent me" (Jn. 4, 34).

Prophetic Intervention in the History of Man

AMOS

1 The book which records the visions and oracles of Amos gives us hardly any details about the prophet's life. He was born in the little town of Tekoa, fifty miles south of Bethlehem, and was a herdsman and dresser of sycamore trees. An irresistible voice compelled him to leave everything in order to carry the message of death from Yahveh to the Northern Kingdom. One day at Bethel, the chief sanctuary of the kingdom founded by Jeroboam, he announced that the reigning dynasty would perish by the sword and that Israel would be carried away captive far from her own country. Amasia the chief priest was obliged to silence the prophet and order him to depart from the territory of Samaria. How the episode ended is not known. This is all the information we have about the prophet's life.

The time is the reign of Jeroboam II (783-743), great-grandson of Jehu, just after Israel had come victoriously out of a century long struggle with Syria and had recovered the ancient boundaries of David's kingdom. The prestige of Israel had never been higher, yet before Jeroboam's death a redoubtable warrior king, Tiglath-Pileser III (745-727), had mounted the throne of Assyria and begun the long series of great conquerors who were to make the world tremble. A terrible sword of Damocles was thus suspended over all the small states of Syria and Palestine.

A.—A THUNDERBOLT FROM A SUMMER SKY

Around the middle of the eighth century all was apparently going well in Israel. Damascus had not yet recovered from the blow dealt it a few years previously by the Assyrian king Adad-Nirari III. The kingdom of Samaria under Jeroboam II had taken advantage of her rival's weakness to recover her ancient frontiers from the Dead Sea to the edge of the Beqa plateau. Prosperity and well-being went hand-in-hand with political power. Sudden wealth, however, was not without its effect on the traditional harmony of society. While it accumulated in the hands of a favored few, there was a rapid decline in small hereditary property—the piece of ground of which Naboth's vineyard is a typical example. The peasant proprietor was becoming a tenant while waiting to sell himself as a serf in order to pay his mounting debts. For the first time in the history of the Jewish people we find the social phenomenon of monopoly and concentration of wealth, a process leading inevitably to pauperism. The law ought to have been able to provide a remedy, but the same process brought bribery and corruption in its train. As the rich were satisfied, the people as a whole seemed to be happy, for it is rare for pauperism and the proletarianization of the masses to be adduced as arguments against the prosperity of a country.

The royal summer and winter palaces were lined with ivory and ebony, while the silver in the temples enhanced the pomp and splendor of the processions and liturgical rites. There was the celebration, for instance, of the recent victories of the armies of Israel such as the capture of Lo-Debar and Carnaim (6, 13). At the festival of Yahveh the royal sanctuary of Bethel resounded more than ever with the singing of canticles accompanied by the harp (5, 23). Popular rejoicing was, of course, the rule at religious ceremonies until the time of the Exile; only that now the wine that flowed in the goblets and the oil that perfumed their heads came from the fines extorted from the poor by unscrupulous judges:

Hear this word, women of the mountains of Samaria,
you cows of Bashan,
you who oppress the weak and abuse the needy,
who say to your husbands, "Bring drink for us!" (4, 1)
Upon garments taken in pledge they recline beside
     every altar;
and the wine of those who have been fined
they drink in the house of their god. (2, 8)

But the lavishness of the newly-rich could not hide a malady
which lay deep—the "affliction of Joseph," an affliction from
which the song composers still improvising their songs as in the
time of David appeared to be immune (6, 5-6). For their sense
of well-being is an illusion. The people of God no longer feel the
hand of Yahveh laid upon them. In their quest of wealth they
no longer feel the pricking of the goad. Their awakening was to
be all the ruder when this master's voice suddenly made itself
heard:

Yahveh will roar from Zion,
and from Jerusalem raise his voice. (1, 2)

A thunderbolt from a summer sky, announcement of the approaching storm, a last warning before the general crash. The
people of God had lost the memory of the great design shaping
their destiny. Their one aim is to defend themselves from the
ambitions of their neighbors, and they see their destiny in terms
of diplomatic and military moves in a Syro-Palestinian world
that will last for ever. But it was not for this they had been
created, and Yahveh was about to sweep away with the blast of
a storm the narrow world to which his people had confined their
joys and sorrows, their hopes and fears.

Since the death of Solomon the two kingdoms of Judah and
Samaria had not ceased to oppose the ambition of Damascus

to dominate this corner of the East. In the time of Ahaz, when Damascus was successful against all the Syro-Palestinian kingdoms, the Northern kingdom had had great difficulty in maintaining its independence. Its neighbors had not been slow to take advantage of the situation. The Philistines had attacked Israel and Judah from the rear, while Ammon, Edom and Moab had shaken off the state of vassalage that had been imposed upon them by David's firm hand.

But now all this was finished; such was the decision of Yahveh. He was about to put an end to these conflicts, while princes and gods would take the path of exile:

> For three crimes of Damascus, and for four,
> I will not revoke my word;
> because they threshed Galaad with sledges of iron,
> I will send fire upon the house of Hazel,
> to devour the castles of Ben-Hadad.
> I will break the bar of Damascus;
> I will root out those who live in the Valley of Aven,
> and the sceptered ruler of Beth-Eden;
> the people of Aram shall be exiled to Kir. . . .
> For three crimes of Gaza, and for four, . . .
> I will root out those who live in Ashdod,
> and the sceptered ruler of Ascalon;
> I will turn my hand against Ekron,
> and the last of the Philistines shall perish. . . .
> For three crimes of Tyre, and for four . . .
> because they delivered whole groups captive in Edom,
> and did not remember the pact of brotherhood. . . .
> For three crimes of Edom and for four . . .
> because he pursued his brother with the sword,
> choking up all pity;
> because he persisted in his anger,
> and kept his wrath to the end. . . .
> For three crimes of the Ammonites, and for four . . .

because they ripped open expectant mothers in Galaad,
while extending their territory. . . .
For three crimes of Moab, and for four. . . .
I will send fire upon Moab,
to devour the castles of Kerioth;
Moab shall meet death and uproar
and shouts and trumpet blasts.
I will root out the judge from her midst,
and her princes I will slay with him. (1, 3-2, 3)

The ground has been cleared, and nothing is left around Israel. She stands alone before her God, and must necessarily raise her eyes towards him. After disposing of all her neighbors, Yahveh is coming to judge his people, the people he led out of Egypt and across the desert (2, 10). He had given them prophets and Nazarites as guides, but they had given the Nazarites wine to drink and closed the mouths of the prophets (2, 11-12). This time Israel will not escape punishment. They will be rooted to the ground and no one shall save his life, neither the valiant nor the swift of foot nor the horseman (2, 13-15).

The people of the Covenant had fallen asleep in a little world shut up in itself, concerned only with its intrigues with its neighbors. But the hand of God imposes continuous activity and movement upwards, and does not tolerate long comfortable pauses, a settling down into immobility. Israel was far from suspecting that she would be rudely dragged into the struggles of great empires. Blinded by her temporary prosperity, she refused to take notice of the great black cloud rising in the north, where the irresistible power of Assyria was preparing to sweep down along the whole coast as far as the Nile valley. Yahveh had set his people at the crucial point where the clash was inevitable between the two empires of Babylonia and Egypt from which civilization had sprung. At a period in history when things were quiet the Hebrews had been able to fix their home in a land where it would be impossible for them to remain on indefinitely. The fall of the Hittite empire and the invasion of Egypt by the sea peoples at the time of Ramses III had left an empty space in which, after the Philistines, the tribes of Israel had settled. Sooner or later the open jaws of the vice would close again. And now midway through the eighth century the hour had struck. The judgment of Yahveh had been pronounced.

While all around is collapsing in ruin, Israel in the hands of her God enters upon a new phase of her history. Gone are the quarrels with Damascus and her other neighbors; the Assyrian colossus is now towering above her, and it is against this she has to fight for life. Thus she now enters on the stage of world history, and her destiny gradually merges into that of all mankind. The voice of the prophet is lifted up in the middle of the eighth century to announce not the end of the world, but the end of *a* world.

B.—A THREAT OF DEATH

Amos, naturally, was not privileged to see the full accomplishment of God's design. He was able to announce that the history of the chosen people was about to acquire a new and unexpected breadth, but only one act of the drama was clear to him, the disaster that was about to overwhelm them and apparently destroy them. The threat of death hanging over the kingdom of Samaria is the theme that dominates and explains all the prophetic utterances of this herdsman from Tekoa.

His mission was the outcome of a series of visions. It should be noted that the visions were not necessarily connected with dreams. Any real ordinary incident could have been the cause of them, provided it opened up fresh knowledge of the divine mystery to the man of God. Whether sleeping or waking, Amos found himself faced at every turn with the fatal menace. He could see a whole series of disasters ready to strike at the kingdom in spite of its full tide of prosperity. Vision follows vision, and each confirms the irrevocable doom.

Thus, in the season when the grass is beginning to grow again after the first mowing, and the hay has already been requisitioned by the royal superintendents, the prophet in a dream sees an invasion of clouds of locusts, spelling ruin for the peasant, and he exclaims compassionately:

Forgive, O Lord Yahveh!
How can Jacob stand? He is so small! (7, 2)

After this first nightmare has passed, another follows. A devouring fire dries up springs and fountains and scorches the earth. Again Amos intercedes and entreats, and Yahveh relents (7, 4-6).

But the condemnation is heard again, insistently. A man is holding a plumbline against a wall. The prophet at once recognizes the line for what it is, a line for dividing up the land of Israel—war, defeat and devastation are at hand. And this time Amos dares not intervene because he knows that Yahveh will not relent (7, 7-9). A basket of ripe fruit, with a play on words in Hebrew between "ripe fruit" and "end," fills him with the gloomiest forebodings. Once before, one fatal night, Yahveh had sent a plague to sow desolation in every Egyptian dwelling, and now he is coming to accomplish the work of destruction among his own people (8, 1-3). There will be no lack of work for the gravediggers, the ground will be strewn with corpses:

If one says to a man inside a house,
"Is anyone with you?"
and he answers, "No one,"
then he shall say, "Silence!"
for no one must mention the name of Yahveh. (6, 10)

Some time later the herdsman from Tekoa goes to Bethel, the great royal sanctuary. While the crowd is given over to the merrymaking that accompanies the religious rites, the prophet sees an arm raised above the altar and hears a command from Yahveh: to strike the pillar heads and let the roof fall in (9, 1).

The blow that is about to fall will destroy everything, for by striking the temple, the center and pivot of the world, it will inevitably crush the whole nation.

There is death in the air. The Western mind, especially in the modern age, may find it difficult to grasp the full force of the images of violence of which the Book of Amos is full. They do not seem to add intensity to the sentence of destruction, but for Israel the word "death" alone would not have been enough to evoke the idea of complete annihilation. Shock at the horror of death was a normal reaction of mankind from earliest times, but it was at the death of another, the rigidity of the corpse lying there on the ground. The Egyptians, for example, refusing to face the problem, walled up and petrified life in the pyramids, thinking to prolong it indefinitely in the silence of blocks of stone.

But for Amos it was quite a different matter. He has an intuition of *existential* death, a death perceived by the subject himself, *my* death, the sudden and irrevocable ending of *my* living force. He evoked the image of it from the inside, it might be said. Israel's experience would not be to become a decaying corpse, an unrecognizable skeleton, but to feel the ground giving way under the feet while dreams faded, plans and calculations failed, the deepest aspirations of existence were extinguished, and the lifegiving sap dried up.

Amos could have told Amasia the priest quite simply, "You shall die on such a day," but the effect of the threat would have been much less impressive than that which his prophecy could not fail to produce:

Now thus says Yahveh:
Your wife shall be made a harlot in the city,
and your sons and daughters shall fall by the sword;
your land shall be divided by measuring line,
and you yourself shall die in an unclean land;
Israel shall be exiled far from its land. (7, 17)

All that the unfortunate man's life is made up of will melt away before his eyes. His wife, whose presence is the guarantee of a stable existence, will be the first to disappear, reduced to a shameful state worse than death. Then he will lose his sons and daughters through whom he would have survived and his name been perpetuated. Finally the earth itself, instead of receiving and guarding his bones, will abandon him. Uprooted from his soil and stricken with eternal barrenness, like the trees of which Yahveh destroyed the fruit above and the roots beneath (2, 9), he will be cast away and left to rot on hostile ("unclean") soil.

Here the intuition of death in Amos is at its strongest. Death is essentially a falling, as life is a rising:

She is fallen, to rise no more, the Virgin Israel;
she lies abandoned upon her land,
with not one to raise her up. (5, 2)

Like Jephte's daughter, the Virgin Israel bewails her useless virginity as a fleeting dream. The man of mature age sees ruin bringing the failure of the hopes he had placed in the labor of his hands. Strangers will dwell in the fine house of hewn stone that the villager has built for himself, and drink the wine of the pleasant vineyards he has planted (5, 11). The invader will reap the harvest of the land bestowed on her by Yahveh that Israel has toiled to render fruitful. The prophecy with which the book ends seeks to attenuate the anguish born of the terrible judgment:

I will bring about the restoration of my people Israel;
they shall rebuild and inhabit their ruined cities,
plant vineyards and drink the wine,
set out gardens and eat the fruits. (9, 14)

But elsewhere Amos utterly dashes all hopes of seeing a reward to an effort blessed by God. The death he announces is the collapse of all that a man holds dear, has desired or created at the expense of unceasing labor.

Another image with the same idea is the dawning day which calls spontaneously to mind the hopes springing from the human heart. In ancient Egypt all religious aspirations were focused around the triumphal rising of the sun. Hope-empty darkness symbolized the finality of death:

> What will this day of Yahveh mean for you?
>   Darkness and not light! (5, 18)
> On that day, says the Lord Yahveh,
> I will make the sun set at midday,
> and cover the earth with darkness in broad daylight.
> I will turn your feasts into mourning,
> and all your songs into lamentations. (8, 9-10)

This is certainly not the gentle obscurity in which tired eyes repose when they are shut, but a gloomy, mournful night that swallows up and delivers a man dazed and defenseless over to a monster-peopled darkness:

> As if a man were to flee from a lion,
> and a bear should meet him;
> or if on entering his house he were to rest his hand
>   against the wall,
> and a snake should bite him.
> Will not the day of Yahveh be darkness and not light
> gloom without any brightness? (5, 19-20)

The death the prophet announces is no repose that nothing will ever disturb, the repose of a soul bruised by life, but a shrinking, a choking, the fear and trembling of a hunted man, a nightmare flight of terror and anguish in which the feet are suddenly rooted to the ground:

Beware, I will crush you into the ground
as a wagon crushes when laden with sheaves.
Flight shall perish from the swift,
and the strong man shall not retain his strength;
the warrior shall not save his life,
nor the bowman stand his ground;
the swift of foot shall not escape,
nor the horseman save his life,
and the most stouthearted of warriors shall flee
    naked on that day. (2, 13-16)

There is no gleam of hope for the condemned. Israel shall
wander in vain from sea to sea in search of a word from her God
and shall not find it (8, 11-12). She will be quite helpless and
her ruin will be complete:

As the shepherd snatches from the mouth of the lion
a pair of legs or the tip of an ear of his sheep,
so shall escape the Israelites. (3, 12)

To emphasize the realism of his threat the prophet describes
its tragic progression: famine (4, 6), drought (4, 8), other disasters to agriculture (4, 9), plague (4, 10), war (4, 10), and
finally, an earthquake to take the ground from under their feet
(4, 11). Dying does not mean leaving the world but feeling one
is being left by it.

But though everything deserts Israel, something still remains.
Yahveh's hand has not loosened its hold and his people cannot
escape from it. Whatever may happen, there is an underlying
sense of death leading inevitably to a meeting with an avenging
God:

Though they break through to the nether world,
even from there my hand shall bring them out;

though they climb to the heavens,
I will bring them down;
though they hide on the summit of Carmel,
there too I will hunt them out and take them away;
though they hide from my gaze in the bottom of the sea.
I will command the serpent there to bite them;
though they are led into captivity by their enemies,
there will I command the sword to slay them.
I will fix my gaze upon them for evil and not for good. (9,2-4)

There is nowhere hope or way of escape.

Prepare to meet your God, O Israel! (4, 12)

C.—SEEK ME AND YOU SHALL LIVE

In the middle of this eighth century before Christ, then, Israel was due for a rough awakening. The question was whether the sentence was to be final. By the mouth of his prophet the God of hosts answers, "Seek the Lord that you may live" (5, 6).

What does this "Seek the Lord" mean? Was not his worship carried out in the sanctuaries? Were not the ritual ties uniting man with the deity observed with the greatest care?

The seeking which Amos speaks of was something quite different from this. It takes on an entirely new meaning, one on which the Bible was to insist right up to the gospel of St. John. To seek God is to be and to remain at the disposal of the Lord of history, to be at one with his will.

The gods of antiquity were kept in an enclosed space, inviolable and jealously guarded. Their world was surrounded by an aura of mystery and aloofness, like a fairy world in a child's imagination. Guardian spirits strictly forbade access to the sacred precinct. Only the charmed word could obtain an entry, such as the formulas that allowed a priest or a Pharaoh to identify himself with his gods. All dealings with them were introduced by the artifice of ritual words and gestures to which a kind of magical effect was attributed. The ancient Egyptian *Book of the Dead* is a perfect illustration of this. Man's approach to God was thus subject to regulations which were all the stricter because they were felt to be arbitrary. Any real dialogue between God and man hardly existed.

When at length the dialogue did take place, the day that God himself took the initiative, man's role was limited to listening as an obedient servant. For the people of the Covenant, seeking God was no longer to consist in multiplying rites and sacrifices, but in submitting their destiny to the transcendent design of Yahveh:

> With what shall I come before Yahveh,
> and bow before God most high?
> Shall I come before him with holocausts,
> with calves a year old?
> You have been told, O man, what is good,
> and what the Lord requires of you:
> Only to do the right and to love goodness,
> and to walk humbly with your god. (Micah 6, 6-8)

But Israel was no longer seeking God in purity of heart. It had forgotten the sense of the quest that was to have been its greatness. Now that God was threatening it with his vengeance, the easiest way to ward off the danger was to build altars and sanctuaries in which the divine name would be invoked and the cry rise incessantly, "Yahveh with us!" How can they not see that worship such as this is vain and deceitful, and that the hope that inspires it is a fatal illusion?

> Seek me that you may live,
> but do not seek Bethel;
> do not come to Galgal,
> and do not cross to Bersheba.
> For Galgal shall be led into exile,

2

and Bethel shall become nought. (5, 4-5)
Those who swear, "By the life of your god, O Dan!"
and "By the life of your love, O Bersheba!"
those shall fall, never to rise again. (8, 14)

All is ready, however, for the traditional ceremonies, the next
day's sacrifice, the offering to follow. The roads to the places
of pilgrimage are thronged with joyful crowds. On the way they
meet with a kill-joy, the herdsman from Tekoa who jeers at them:

Go to Bethel and sin,
to Galgal and sin even more!
Each morning bring your sacrifices,
every third day your tithes.
Burn leavened food as a thanksgiving sacrifice,
proclaim publicly your freewill offerings,
for so you love to do, O men of Israel. (4, 4-5)

Respectable people at the time must have resented his language. When so many of the population were deserting the high
places, they probably argued, was it wise to discourage the faithful ones, whose generosity safeguarded the continuance of public worship? But whoever had ventured to raise an objection
would have received a blunt answer from Amos:

Seek good and not evil,
that you may live;
then truly will Yahveh, the God of hosts, be with you
    as you claim!
Hate evil and love good,
and let justice prevail at the gate;
then it may be that Yahveh, the God of hosts,
will have pity on the remnant of Joseph. (5, 14-15)

Nor can Israel be any longer sure of the promise that seemed
to be renewed in the autumn festivals. Every year, at the first

rains that sent up the dust from the parched fields, the people would acclaim their faith not only in the earth's renewal but also in the beginning of a new age. Since the autumn festival was held at the same time as that of the kingship of Yahveh, they must have had all the more reason to remember that his kingship extended over the whole country, and they must have doubtless hoped to obtain peace and security from Yahveh as the price of their devotion. During these feast days the liturgy glorified the national God, who had created both the earth and the heavens, and affirmed its certainty that the world would arise anew from chaos, and a dazzling light from the darkness.

But the gladness of these feast days was about to be changed into mourning:

> In every vineyard there shall be lamentation
> when I pass through your midst, says Yahveh. (5, 17)

There can be no hope for the future as long as there is no change in behavior:

> Woe to those who yearn for the day of Yahveh!
> What will this day of Yahveh mean for you?
> Darkness and not light! (5, 18)

For the people that refuses to understand, terrible indeed will be the dawning of the day of Yahveh. The God who thunders through the voice of Amos will have about him nothing of the King at whose yearly coming there was a renewal of optimism:

> You will carry away the tent of your King . . .
> for I will exile you beyond Damascus. (5, 26-27)[1]

---

1. The Confraternity Edition gives the reading for this rather difficult verse as "You will carry away Sakkuth, your king, and Kaiwan, your star god." Sikkut and Kaiwan were not among the most famous of the Babylonian gods, and it is doubtful whether they were even known in eighth

It is useless for Israel to seek reassurance and protection by invoking the ancient pact, the Covenant of Sinai. That agreement was bilateral, and Yahveh is under no obligation to keep his side of the bargain. If in former times he chose Israel out from among all other nations, he is still free to revoke his choice:

> Are you not like the Ethiopians to me, O men of Israel?
> Did I not bring the Israelites from the land of Egypt
> as I brought the Philistines from Caphtor and the
>   Arameans from Kir?
> My eyes are on this sinful kingdom;
> I will destroy it from off the face of the earth. (9, 7-8)

Yahveh will act as he thinks fit towards the people he has chosen. He may bless them or punish them, grant or withhold his favors from them, send death or abundance of life. Whatever the circumstances, his sovereign power will not be affected by their victory or defeat. He has nothing in common with other gods like Melkom, Melkart, Hadad or Chamos, whose fate was bound up with that of the nations who adored them. Yahveh would still survive even if Israel were to disappear, for the initiative of the choice was his. He would therefore never bow before the whims of his chosen people but always remain an exacting Master to be served with respect!

> You alone have I favored, more than all the families
>   of the earth;
>   therefore I will punish you for all your crimes. (3, 2)

---

century Israel. It seems strange that a man such as Amos should have tried to make a parade of learning by quoting their names. The Septuagint reading appears to be the more likely one, taking "sikkût" (cf. Douay Version, "You carried a tabernacle for your Moloch"). The text is a simple allusion to the feast of Yahveh the King, **Yahveh Melek** (transcribed as **Moloch** in Greek), a title which Yahveh refuses to accept, as later he refuses to accept that of Baal (Hos. 2, 18).

It is useless, therefore, to multiply offerings or nourish a presumptuous faith in a repetition of divine favors, as if they were as inevitable and regular as the return of the seasons. The hand of Yahveh cannot be forced. He is neither a blind force of nature nor a susceptible potentate to be rendered harmless or lulled to sleep by empty flattery. The glib language of hollow praise can be left to devotees of the gods of Babylon. The God of Israel is the God of history. He had reserved the Hebrews for the accomplishment of a design which was the only thing that mattered in his eyes. To obtain his favor it was necessary to walk in his ways: "It is love I desire, not sacrifice" (Hos. 6, 6; cf. 1 Sam. 15, 22)—"Not everyone who says to me, 'Lord, Lord' shall enter the kingdom of heaven, but he who does the will of my father in heaven" (Matt. 7, 21).

The will of the Father was to be translated by Christianity essentially into the charter of love, but now eight centuries before the Gospel Amos lets us catch a glimpse of its message by placing foremost among God's requirements the maintenance of the spirit of brotherhood that had formerly marked the unity of the people of the covenant. Social injustice, barefaced fraud, bribery of judges are some of the things that for him are violations of the pact of Sinai. Let the rich give up their life of luxury and the powerful cease from their abuse of power, and only then will the cry of his people be heard by Yahveh:

I hate, I spurn your feasts,
I take no pleasure in your solemnities;
your cereal offerings I will not accept,
nor consider your stall-fed peace offerings.
Away with your noisy songs!
I will not listen to the melodies of your harps.
But if you would offer me holocausts,
then let justice surge like water,
and goodness like an unfailing stream. (5, 21-24)

Otherwise the rash confidence of a people who think they are well-off will meet with inexorable punishment:

By the sword shall all sinners among my people die,
those who say, "Evil will not reach or overtake us." (9, 10)

Far from placating him, all the noisy demonstrations of a hypocritical worship will only serve to increase Yahveh's wrath and hasten the hour of judgment:

You would put off the evil day,
yet you hasten the reign of violence. (6, 3)

There is only one way open to Israel, that of obedience: "Seek God and you shall live!"

HOSEA

2 Hosea, the son of Beeri, was a native of the Northern Kingdom. Few details of his life are known, and these are still the subject of discussion. Two accounts, one from the hand of the prophet himself (chapter 3), the other from that of one of his disciples (chapter 1) seem to refer to the same episode: his marriage to a sacred prostitute named Gomer.

The prophet lived through the events which convulsed the last days of the Northern Kingdom. After six months' reign Jeroboam's son Zechariah was assassinated (743) and was succeeded in turn by Shallum, Menahem, Pekahiah, Pekah and Hosea until the day Samaria finally fell to Sargon II after a three year siege (721). Damascus had already fallen ten years earlier (732).

The book is extremely difficult in places, the text being one of the most badly preserved of the Old Testament, so that interpretation is often guesswork.

A.—CONSPIRACY AND REVOLUTION

In the thirty-eighth year of Azariah king of Judah, Zechariah the son the Jeroboam reigned over Israel of Samaria for six months (2 Kings 15, 8). Shallum the son of Jabesh conspired against him, and smote him before the people, and slew him, and reigned in his stead (15, 10). He reigned for a month in Samaria. Menahem the son of Gadi went up from Tirzah and came to Samaria, and smote Shallum the son of Jabesh in Samaria, and slew him, and reigned in his stead (15, 13-14). Pekahiah the son of Menahem reigned over Israel in Samaria for two years. . . . Pekah the son of Remaliah, his captain, conspired against him, and smote him in Samaria, in the tower of the king's house . . . and he slew him and reigned in his stead (15, 23-25). Hoshea the son of Elah made a conspiracy against Pekah the son of Remaliah, and smote him, and slew him, and reigned in his stead (15, 30).

A series of *coups d'état* in such rapid succession was something new in Samaria. The monarchy in the Northern Kingdom was no doubt much less stable than in Judah, where the dynasty of David had obtained an assurance of perpetuity from Yahveh. But mere ambition on the part of a few adventurers would not have been enough to cause so many palace revolutions. An explanation must be found in the strong currents of public opinion that divided and shook the country. While the Omrides, for example, occupied the throne, they had tried to carry through a Mediterranean policy of alliance with Tyre to offset the attempts of Damascus to become the dominant power. Against this, Jehu's *pronunciamento* was a result of the prophets' reaction to the growing influence of Phoenicia. But now the changes follow each other at such a rate that none of the new rulers remains in power long enough to be able to impose a stable foreign policy. And one good reason for the uncertainty and vacillation which was typical of the state of the country was the fear inspired by Tiglath-Pileser whose army was encamped on its frontiers.

The problem was whether the small Syro-Palestinian states should form a league against the Assyrian menace. A century earlier the experiment had partially succeeded. The solution could not fail to gain wide support, but in the end it proved to be a disastrous one. The members of the coalition were put out of action one by one. Hamat in the north was the first victim.

In a panic Menahem thought it wise to come to terms with the
Assyrians, but popular opposition to his policy brought about
his downfall. Meanwhile Damascus took the lead in a new anti-
Assyrian league and was trying to get the kingdom of Jerusalem
to join it. The affair ended badly for her; in 732 the proud city
of the Ben-Hadads fell to the Assyrians never to rise again.

The only state left in active opposition was Samaria, already
shorn of part of her territory. It was necessary for a new govern-
ment to negotiate a peace, which had to be bought on hard
terms with the recognition of Assyria as overlord. This did not
prevent King Hoshea some years later from joining in a general
revolt on the occasion of the Assyrian conqueror's death, but the
latter's successor, Salmanasar V, was not slow in reasserting his
power. Realizing that his position was definitely compromised,
Hoshea took the bold step of appealing for the first time to the
only power capable of stemming the Assyrian tidal wave and
made an alliance with Egypt. This desperate decision was followed by a ruthless repression. In 721 the Northern Kingdom disappeared for ever from the stage of history. A quarter of a century had not yet passed before the prophecy of Amos had proved
true.

During this short period the helm had passed from hand
to hand and the ship had been kept afloat as best it could, until
it had struck against the fatal rock and been submerged. The surprising thing is the patience the Assyrians seem to have shown
towards Israel in allowing a vassal state so much liberty in deciding foreign policy. Actually, more than a matter of patience, it
was a question of waiting for the right moment for the cat to
pounce on the mouse. The Assyrian empire was not in a position
to exert constant pressure everywhere at the same time. Faced
with a war on two fronts, it would strike alternately to the east
and to the west, thus giving the enemy a breathing space to re-
cuperate and nourish the vain illusion that there was still some
hope.

At the height of the storm, however, a voice was there to point out the way to safety. Through the mouth of the prophet Hosea, Yahveh's voice could be heard protesting against the sudden changes in policy and the continual *coups d'état*. "They have made kings, but not by my authority" (8, 4); "Ephraim is like a dove, silly and senseless" (7, 11), flying tentatively now towards Egypt, now towards Assyria:

> Ephraim chases the wind,
> ever pursuing the gale.
> His lies and falsehoods are many;
> He comes to terms with Assyria,
> and carries oil to Egypt. (12, 2)

It is a state of incoherence that is dangerous in the circumstances and soon to become fatal—because they have sown the wind, they shall reap the whirlwind (8, 7). Wherever they look for help, it will only serve to hasten their ruin. Alliance with Egypt or submission to Assyria, either solution will only save appearances. Whether the country exhausts itself with voluntary gifts or is ruined by paying tribute, it is heading for disaster:

> Ephraim mingles with the nations,
> Ephraim is a hearth cake unturned.
> Strangers have sapped his strength,
> but he takes no notice of it;
> of gray hairs, too, there is a sprinkling,
> but he takes no notice of it. (7, 8-9)

So what is to be done? They would know if they hearkened to the prophet's voice who with finger outstretched points out the way:

> I am Yahveh, your God, since the land of Egypt;

you know no God besides me,
and there is no savior but me. (13, 4)

But in the general confusion Israel has now lost all awareness
of the sense of her history, or of even being under God's hand:

Israel has forgotten his maker. (8, 14)

Who brought them out from bondage in Egypt? Who guided,
fed and sustained them in the desert? Who has ever since shaped
their destiny? Who has always watched over them with a father's
care?

When Israel was a child, I loved him,
out of Egypt I called my son. (11, 1)

It was I who taught Ephraim to walk,
who took him in my arms. (11, 3)

I stooped to feed my child. (11, 4)

The reminder of his loving presence is all the more moving
now that Israel is in her death agony. But is it Yahveh who
should awaken the memory of it in the fickle hearts of his people? In the hour of danger there is no man who does not think
of the mother who fondled and protected him in childhood, or
instinctively seeks solace and refuge in the arms no longer there
to welcome him. Though God had given his people much more
than a mother gives her son and still remained close to them,
Israel would not think of turning to him if he himself by the
mouth of the prophet did not remind them of his love.
    The story of this forgotten love is as stirring and dramatic
as any to be found in the stories of the world. It had begun in
the desert:

Like grapes in the desert, I found Israel;
like the first fruits of the fig tree in its prime,
I considered your fathers. (9, 10).

Yahveh had rejoiced in these first fruits, as the Beduin delights in the fig that refreshes him. What things he hoped for
from his people responsive to him!

Ephraim is a trained heifer,
willing to tread out the corn;
I myself will lay a yoke upon her fair neck;
Ephraim will be harnessed,
Judah will plow,
Jacob will break his furrows.
Sow for your selves justice,
reap the fruit of piety,
break up for yourselves a new field,
for it is time to seek Yahveh. (10, 11-12)

But how bitter the fruit of the covenant was to become!

Why have you cultivated wickedness,
reaped perversely,
and eaten the fruit of falsehood? (10, 13)

Yahveh, a jealous God, demanded total surrender into his hands
and exclusive love, but Israel had despised his tenderness and
sought everywhere else for the assistance that only their God
could give them. They had thought that they could rely on their
own resources, the help of their neighbors, or the forces of nature.
For their safety they had counted their chariots and warriors, had
made fragile human pacts when they had the majestic power
of the Covenant, and had fashioned idols with which they hoped
to subjugate the other pagan divinities:

Woe to them, for they have strayed far from me! (7, 13)

The malady, however, is not incurable. It is only her infidelity which has made Israel sick, but they must not delay longer in acknowledging their error:

Assyria will not save us,
nor shall we have horses to mount;
we shall say no more, "Our god,"
to the work of our hands. (14, 3)

On these terms Israel may still have hope:

You shall return by the help of your God,
if you remain loyal and do right
and always hope in your God. (12, 6)

B.—A GOD OF LOVE OR BAAL

Israel was not the plaything of some blind force, but was destined to serve the great design of God. Amos had already vigorously emphasized this idea; Hosea now presents it from a fresh angle, giving it an added importance from the imminent downfall of Samaria. He shows that this design of God is a *design of love*. It is true that Yahveh insists that Israel should remember the mighty hand that has always guided them:

I am Yahveh, your God, since the land of Egypt. (12, 9; 13, 4)

But this is not enough. The other peoples, too, remember their national gods. What he wishes is that Israel should not forget the love which has been shown them:

When Israel was a child, I loved him. (11, 1)

I drew them with cords, of kindness,
    with bands of love. (11, 4)

This love desires repayment.
It is love that I desire. (6, 6)

*   *   *

Most commentators are agreed that one of the main objects of
the prophets was to extirpate worship of the false gods from the
holy nation. All the prophetic writings seem to point to this. They
are full of scathing attacks against the worship in the "high
places" which, though officially paid to Yahveh, was yet contami-
nated by polytheism and idolatry. But without denying that this
was also one of their objectives, we should be wrong in seeing
the prophets as mere preachers of monotheism in the style, for
instance, of Mahomet. The monotheism of the Bible is not just
a question of number, a choice betwen a dozen or so gods and
a single one. The problem is a much deeper one and essentially
concerns the nature of the relations of man with the Godhead.

It could be formulated thus: Was Yahveh to be considered as
a *Baal*, that is as the owner of the land, the fertilizer of the soil,
the provider of food for man and beast, or as a *loving will*, sum-
moning his people to let itself be guided by what he desired? In
the first case, the chosen people would have done enough, under
the cover of the name of their God, to ensure salvation by
observing the ritual and ceremonies designed to obtain renewal
of the forces of nature. In the second there could be no other
religion for Israel but a response through *obedience* and *fidelity*
to the will of the God who loved them.

This was precisely the problem that Hosea was to solve. If
Israel had gone astray, it was because she had not clearly realized
the originality of her relations with Yahveh and the exchange
of love that was offered her. All that they retained at first from
the divine message was what fitted in most easily with the common beliefs of the peoples in whose midst they lived, and thus
there was a risk at the same time of indiscriminately adopting
outlooks and attitudes repugnant to the faith God demanded of

them. This risk was to prove fatal, as they could not thereby avoid two gross errors: either to reduce Yahveh to a mere force of nature, or to the status of a national king, a tribal god.

With regard to the first, we should take note that their comparatively recent nomadic life had left the Israelites with the idea of the *deus parens,* who "opens the womb" and presides over the growth of the tribe and its herds. In this they were only mindful of Yahveh's conditional promise to Abram, "Be perfect . . . and I will multiply you exceedingly" (Gen. 17, 1-2). The prophet refers to this when he threatens that Israel will be deprived of her fertility by Yahveh ("the glory of Ephraim"):

The glory of Ephraim will fly away like a bird:
no birth, no carrying in the womb, no conception. (9, 11)

To this idea of *deus parens,* which none of the other nomadic tribes would have rejected, another was added, a much more dangerous one, which Israel was to adopt when the nomadic life was forgotten and it had settled down in Canaan as cultivators of the soil, and it began to think mainly of its crops.

As long as they thought that, in accordance with their deserts, Yahveh gave or withheld his blessing on the harvest, they did not go too far wrong. It was in the things that were of most importance to them that they most felt Yahveh's hand. Hosea reminds them of this even when foretelling the disasters to come:

They sow the wind, they shall reap the whirlwind;
the stalk of grain shall form no ear and shall yield no flour;
even if it could, strangers would swallow it. (8, 7)

Or, contrariwise, he points to the rains as a sign and symbol of God's favor:

He will revive us after two days;
on the third day he will raise us up,
to live in his presence.

Let us know, let us strive to know Yahveh;
as certain as the dawn is his coming. . . .
He will come to us like the rain,
like spring rain that waters the earth. (6, 2-3)

But when the harvest fails and, like all countrymen, they
feel the heartache which could be salutary for them, it does not
follow that Yahveh is a divinity whose favor it is enough to know
how to gain in order, automatically, to have a good harvest. The
idea of the *deus parens* can be seen here sliding almost im-
perceptibly into that of the Baal of the Phoenicians, the
Babylonian Marduk, the Sumerian Tammuz, and other gods like
Adonis and Cybele. It becomes completely transformed when the
forces of nature are seen, apparently, to be periodically exhausted. Every year the rains stop watering the earth, the springs
dry up, and the grass withers. It appears as if some divinity
whose duty it is to keep the countryside in life is dying. The
peasants despair at this spectacle is to be found in all Oriental
religions, and Israel was no exception:

They wail upon their beds;
for wheat and wine they lacerate themselves. (7, 14)

Songs of mourning were sung in the high places in honor of
the god who was presumed to be dead. But the people were
not content with assisting as mourning and resigned spectators
at the annual drama of nature's death. In the hope of a future
resurrection they would call on the sleeping god and endeavor
themselves to help in the renewal of fertility by giving the exhausted world something of their own living force. This is why

On the mountaintops they offer sacrifice
and on the hills they burn incense,
beneath oak and poplar and terebinth. (4, 13)

There was only one step from this to adopting all the rites intended to favor the return of life, especially that of sacred prostitution, which was considered the most effective. So Israel did not hestitate to graft on to the worship of Yahveh the institution of the *theodules* to symbolize the fruitful union of the national god with the goddess of life.

Yahveh could not but refuse to accept a worship of this kind. It is to be noticed, however, that he is less incensed at the immorality of these practices than by the attempt to force his hand, as if he were Baal whose power of fecundation could be stimulated. His gifts are distributed freely and He needs no help in bestowing them. So He reminds them in what way his unfaithful people should pray to him:

She shall call me "My husband,"
and never again "My Baal."
Then will I remove from her mouth the names of the Baals,
so that they shall no longer be invoked. (2, 16-17)

Otherwise their prayer is a sacrilege if

they do not cry to me from their hearts . . .
but they rebel against me. (7, 14)

He denies any religious meaning to sacred prostitution; in His eyes it is no different from ordinary prostitution:

If your daughters play the harlot,
and your daughters-in-law are adulteresses,
am I then to punish your daughters for their harlotry,
your daughters-in-law for their adultery?
You yourselves consort with harlots,
and with prostitutes you offer sacrifice! (4, 13-14)

The other rites are not much better either, and even the flesh of the sacrifices is in itself of no more value than the meat eaten at home:

> Though they offer sacrifice, immolate flesh and eat it,
> Yahveh is not pleased with them. (8, 13)

Yahveh is not a *Baal*, but neither is he a national king. Among peoples of a firmly settled way of life such as were to be found in Egypt, Babylonia and Canaan, the institution of monarchy seemed a guarantee of nature's periodical return. The monarchy was held to be the god-king's vicar to whom was entrusted the task of ensuring for his people the stable and peaceful posses- sion of their land. Each new reign, as each new year, was the occasion for reaffirming the kingship of the national god.

Israel had to accept these usages of the surrounding lands. Yahveh's annual festival about which the Bible speaks was, in all probability, one and the same as that of national kingship. In any case, the proclamation of this kingship was at the origin of the expectation of a new era, the hope of a new creation in which wars of men with men and with a hostile nature would cease, a dream of universal harmony when heaven itself would be recon- ciled with earth:

> I will make a covenant for them on that day
> with the beasts of the field, with the birds of the air,
> and with the things that crawl on the ground.
> Bow and sword and war I will destroy from the land,
> and I will let them take their rest in security. (2, 18)

> On that day I will respond to the heavens,
> and they shall respond to the earth;
> the earth shall respond to the grain, and wine, and oil,
> and these shall respond to Jezrael. (2, 21-22)

But it is only unwillingly that the institution of monarchy in Israel has been tolerated by Yahveh!

I give you a king in my anger,
and I take him away in my wrath. (13, 11)

His objection to monarchy is quite understandable from the
significance that was bound to be attached to it. By proclaiming
Yahveh's kingship they would be inclined to try to have him
intervene, instead of entrusting themselves to his will alone. His
repeated veto on images of any kind was for the same reason, for
fear that they might begin to imagine that the power of their
God was with them in the image and because of it. The other
nations were free to call upon their chief divinity under the
appearance of a bull, the symbol of fecundity and life, but
Yahveh refuses to recognize himself in the golden calf made
by Israel.

Cast away your calf, O Samaria!
My wrath is kindled against them. (8, 5; cf. 8, 6)

He will not accept the role of king they want Him to play,
and exclaims in irritation:

Assyria shall be their king! (11, 5)

How could He be pleased with the hopes that were so rashly
placed in Him?

The inhabitants of Samaria fear for the calf of Beth-Aven;
the people mourn for it, and its priests wail over it,
because the glory has departed from it.
It too shall be carried to Assyria,
as an offering to the great king.
Shame shall fall upon Ephraim,
and Israel shall be confounded for his idol.
Samaria has disappeared!
Her King is like a straw on the surface of the water.
(10, 5-7)

Let Israel not be deceived. Possession of the land, man's fellowship with the soil, universal peace and harmony are gifts that will come only from Yahveh's love. All the ceremonies of the festival of Yahveh are of no avail, and will not prevent the Israelites, guilty of not having hearkened to their God, from becoming "wanderers among the nations" (9, 17), and "like the dew that early passes away, like chaff driven by the wind from the threshing floor or like smoke out of the window" (13, 3); nor their country from being transformed into "a wilderness ravaged by wild beasts" (2, 14).
Then the Israelites

> shall not pour libations of wine to Yahveh,
> or proffer their sacrifices before him.
> Theirs will be like mourners' bread,
> that makes unclean all who eat of it;
> such food as they have shall be for themselves;
> it cannot enter the house of Yahveh. (9, 4)

And Hosea adds with cruel irony:

> What will you do on the festival day,
> the day of Yahveh's feast? (9, 5)

It is only the love of Yahveh which allows Israel to remain on her own soil, so it is useless to multiply rites and sacrifices. Yahveh is neither a baal nor a national god like those of other nations. Israel is asked only that she respond to God's love and remain faithful to the Covenant with him.

> It is love I desire, not sacrifice,
> and knowledge of God rather than holocausts. (6, 6)

Otherwise, if
 there is no fidelity, no mercy, no knowledge of
  God in the land. . . .
 the wind will bind them up in its pinions,
 and they shall have only shame from their altars. (4, 2 & 19)

C.—PURSUIT OF THE HARLOT

 Yahveh's freely-given love demands fidelity on Israel's part. It was at the very moment that he discovered its depth that the prophet became fully aware of the peoples' infidelity its object.

 For the first time in the Bible we now find the allegory of the unfaithful or faithful woman as a symbol of Israel's refusing to give herself to her God. The prostituted nation playing the harlot with her lovers, with the addition of personal touches of a picturesque or realistic nature is a constant theme with the prophets, and had its origin in an event that determined Hosea's mission. In itself it was not very important, but in the special circumstances of its effect upon his vocation it was to have an extraordinary resonance.

 For several hundred years the worship of Yahveh, as we have seen, had become corrupt and tended to become identified with that of the Canaanite gods, one of whose chief features was sacred prostitution. The pure worship of Yahveh, inherited from the desert, must have been ill at ease when in contact with the nature rites of the pagan gods, but so far no one had been able to lay a finger on the exact nature of the evil or point out its full gravity.

 But now the son of Beeri, yielding to some mysterious influence, fell in love with a woman who was a sacred prostitute, and the experience was a revelation to him. He had a sudden intuition that Yahveh, too, in giving his love to Israel, was surrendering it to a harlot. The sacred prostitution in the high places was a clear expression of the same prostitution by which Israel was outraging her God.

> The spirit of harlotry has led them astray;
> they commit harlotry, forsaking their God.
> On the mountaintops they offer sacrifice,
> and on the hills they burn incense,
> beneath oak and poplar and terebinth,
> because of their pleasant shade ...
> (they) consort with harlots,
> and with prostitutes offer sacrifice. (4, 12-14)

The very celebration of the liturgical solemnities was clear evidence of Israel's prostitution, with the young maidens going up to the high places bejewelled and adorned in all their finery like harlots:

> I will punish her for the days of the Baals,
> for whom she burnt incense
> while she decked herself with her rings and her jewels,
> and, in going after her lovers, forgot me. (2, 13)

In the high places they hoped to buy the gift of life, from gods with whom Yahveh had nothing in common and from forces of nature they hailed as gods, and by offerings of fruits of the earth which were only gifts of Yahveh. To try and gain alien support by such means as these was prostitution, as it was prostitution to seek alliances with other nations against Yahveh's will:

> They went up to Assyria —
> a wild ass on its own —
> Ephraim bargained for lovers. (8, 9)

Not one of the tributes paid to gods or men but did not ultimately come from Yahveh's generosity, from the soil he had given and made fruitful. They were like men buying the favors of a mistress with gifts from a wife.

It can be said here that Hosea was not in any way the "Beduin" prophet that some have called him. If, as we shall see later, he preaches a return to the desert, it is not because he despises the land that God has given the Israelites. On the contrary — and this is an essential point in the originality of his message — he sees the gift of the Promised Land as the concrete expression of Yahveh's love for his people. What appears monstrous to him is that Israel should refuse to recognize the proof of his love in the benefits that are daily showered on her:

yes, their mother has played the harlot;
she that conceived them has acted shamefully.
"I will go after my lovers," she said,
"who give me my bread and my water,
my wool and my flax,
my oil and my drink."
She has not known that it was I
who gave her the grain, the wine, and the oil,
and her abundance of silver and of gold,
which they used for Baal. (2, 5-8)

The complaint is as pathetic as it is illuminating. No other people but Israel has ever had a conception of the land it was living in as a wedding gift from a loving God. Where men saw only the automatic working of a cyclic mystery of life, Hosea discerns the sign of divine love in the astonishing adventure which began on the banks of the Nile and ended in Canaan's conquest. The love that Yahveh bears his people, the providential course of its history, the gift of the land from whose fields Israel continues to gather the fruits of the harvest year by year, these are three ideas indivisibly linked which henceforth are clearly emphasized in the Bible and cannot be glossed over without distorting its divine message.

By profaning the gifts of the Covenant, Israel has turned her back on her great history and been false to her God's love:

They ate their fill;
when filled, they became proud of heart
and forgot me. (13, 6)

What treatment will Yahveh mete out to his ungrateful people? Will he leave them to their fate? Will he repudiate them? He would certainly do so, if his tenderness did not speak louder than his justice:

My heart is overwhelmed, my pity is stirred. (11, 8)

He still loves with a personal love the people who have forgotten his benefits to them, so once more he will endeavor to bring back the faithless one:

Therefore I will hedge her way with thorns
and erect a wall against her so that she cannot find her paths.
If she runs after her lovers, she shall not overtake them;
she looks for them she shall not find them.
Then she shall say, "I will go back to my first husband,
for it was better with me then than now." (2, 6-7)

But if, in spite of this, Israel refuses to listen to him, he will say to the rebellious nation:

You are not my people, and I will not be your God. (1, 9)

He will continue to pursue her, if only to take vengeance on her:

I am like a lion to Ephraim,
like a lion's cub to the house of Judah.

It is I who rend the prey and depart,
I carry it away and no one can save it from me. (5, 14)

The decision to punish the guilty one is still an excuse for seeking her out:

Therefore, I will be like a lion to them,
like a panther by the road I will keep watch.
I will attack them like a bear robbed of its young,
and tear their hearts from their breasts. (13, 7-8)

Death itself will be powerless to loosen the grasp of God's hand. However far she falls into the pit of her corruption, the harlot will still retain the indelible imprint of the seal of God's love, the love which, like that which pursues the souls of the damned in spite of their eternal refusal, can know no turning back.

But in His vengeance does Yahveh really desire the death of Israel? Hosea had ransomed Gomer not in order to kill her, but to take her back with him and live with her after a period of trial. His love for her was stronger than his resentment.

D.—RETURN TO THE DESERT

The whole of Israel's history went to prove that Yahveh was not the Baal of the land of Canaan. Had he not formed his people first in Egypt?

I am Yahveh, your God, since the land of Egypt. (13, 4)

He had set his choice on tribes of slaves, despised and hated, with no land of their own and living only on what was given them for their work:

Like grapes in the desert I found Israel. (9, 10)

He had guided them across the desert with a father's care, providing for all their needs and defending them against all dangers:

I fed you in the desert, in the torrid land. (13, 5)

He had come with them into Palestine, the "land of Yahveh" (9, 3), not because he was the tutelary deity of it, but because it was the land he had bestowed on the landless people. He had been just as much their God in the desert as he was in Canaan.

✿   ✿   ✿

Most sedentary peoples have had the experience of a nomad life before settling down in one place, but they have forgotten about it. Israel's originality lay in her remembrance of it; they had never wanted to forget their origin. They seem to have been the only people to recall with pride the time when they possessed nothing but their herds had wandered about in search of pasture. This emotion was no doubt derived from the more or less conscious and avowed remembrance of the God into whose hands their forefathers had entrusted themselves and who had declared to them:

You know no God besides me,
and there is no savior but me. (13, 4)

Nowhere more strongly than in the desert had Israel felt that she was entirely dependent on Yahveh. This fact is strongly emphasized in Deuteronomy:

I led you for forty years in the desert. Your clothes did not fall from you in tatters nor your sandals from your feet; bread was not your food, nor wine or beer your drink. Thus you should know that I, Yahveh, am your God. (Deut. 29, 4-5)

It must not be thought, however, that Israel became resigned reluctantly, as seems to have been the case with Islam, to exchanging a nomadic life for a settled one. The desert was not the theme of popular songs or poetry which sought to keep alive the memory of the past and create a kind of national folklore. If the inspired writers are at pains to preserve the memory of it, they do so in order that the people may appreciate every day of their lives that the gift of God was freely given, and especially that they may never lose the certainty that there is nothing they have not received from the bounty and love of the God who gave them a land flowing with milk and honey for their inheritance. When the pious Israelite went up to the temple to offer the first fruits of the harvest, he would hear the first pages of his people's history read, and this would fill him with a sense of gratitude for what he owed to Yahveh:

> Then you shall declare before Yahveh, your God, "My father was a wandering Aramean who went down to Egypt with a small household and lived there as an alien. But there he became a nation great, strong, and numerous. When the Egyptians maltreated and oppressed us, imposing hard labor upon us, we cried to Yahveh, the God of our Fathers, and he heard our cry and saw our affliction, our toil and our oppression. He brought us out of Egypt with his strong hand and outstretched arm, with terrifying power, with signs and wonders; and bringing us into this country, he gave us this land flowing with milk and honey. Therefore I have now brought you the first fruits of the products of the soil which you, Yahveh, have given me. (Deut. 26, 5-10)

Acknowledgment of God's gift—this apparently simple spiritual attitude was, it would seem, beyond human power for the Israelites, for they came to attribute the fertility of their fields to the magic rites in honor of pagan gods. It may be wondered if there is something exceptional in an aberration such as this. After all, the literature of the world is full of examples of how people in time of prosperity are inclined to place the greatest reliance on their own ability and to forget that in themselves they are nothing and can do nothing:

> They ate their fill; when filled,
> they became proud of heart and forgot me. (13, 6)

To show them the error of their ways, Yahveh will take away everything from them, and the discovery of their wretchedness will be forced upon them:

> I will take back my grain in its time,
> and my wine in its season;
> I will snatch away my wool and my flax,
> with which she covers her nakedness.
> So now I will lay bare her shame before the eyes of her lovers,
> and no one can deliver her out of my hand. . . .
> I will lay waste her vines and fig trees,
> of which she said,
> "These are the hire my lovers have given me."
> I will turn them into rank growth and wild beasts shall
>   devour them. (2, 9-10-12)

Thus Israel, the faithless wife, will find herself alone in her nakedness when she has been stripped of the ornaments and jewels with which she delighted to adorn herself to please her lovers:

> I will strip her naked,
> leaving her as on the day of her birth.
> I will make her like the desert,
> I will reduce her to an arid land. (2, 3)

In other words, Yahveh will bring his people back to its former destitution. There is much more in this than the motive of anger. He will punish it for its ingratitude, to be sure, when he takes back his gifts; but more than this, he will open up a way of salvation for it by imposing a trial of purification, in the same way that, before taking the prostitute Gomer as his wife, Hosea had compelled her to live in continence for a time, according to the usual rite of "de-sacralization":

> "Many days you shall wait for me; you shall not play the harlot or belong to any man; I in turn will wait for you." For the people of Israel shall remain many days without king or prince, without sacrifice or sacred pillar, without ephod or household idols. Then the people of Israel shall turn back and seek Yahveh their God. (3, 3-5)

Yahveh thus offers a last chance to Israel who is dying from her refusal of the love of her God — the chance to find him again in the place of their first meeting, the desolation of the desert:

> I am Yahveh, your God, since the land of Egypt;
> I will again have you live in tents,
> as in that appointed time. (12, 9)

> So I will allure her;
> I will lead her into the desert
> and speak to her heart. (2, 14)

Yahveh's real desire is to reach into Israel's heart. The great drama ends with the marvelous prospect of an idyllic love that nothing will ever afterwards come to trouble. With her hand in her God's, Israel will tread the radiant path of her renewed destiny:

> I will give her back the vineyards she had,
> and the valley of Achor as a door of hope.

She shall respond there as in the days of her youth,
when she came up from the land of Egypt. (2, 15)

I will espouse you to me for ever:
I will espouse you in right and in justice,
in love and in mercy.
I will espouse you in fidelity,
and you shall know Yahveh. (2, 19-20)

Thus, as so often throughout history, the desert with its bareness and privation becomes the symbolic place where the soul can find the living source to heal its sickness.

ISAIAH

3 The Book of Isaiah is much longer than those of Amos and Hosea, but it has been observed for a long time that the writings attributed to him contain a long series of chapters that have nothing to do with the message of this eighth century prophet. This is particularly the case with the second half of the book, from chapter 40 to the end.

A nobleman, not a priest, Isaiah played an important part at the Court of Jerusalem, especially during the reign of the great king Hezekiah (716-687). He tells us himself how he became a prophet. His mission began with a vision in the Temple of Jerusalem the year of King Uzziah's death (740) and lasted until about the year 701.

Two events dominated his career as prophet: the Syro-Ephraimite war (734) and the invasion of Sennacherib (701). The first took place in the reign of Ahaz (736-716), king of Judah. For refusing to enter the coalition against Assyria formed by the kings of Damascus and Samaria, Ahaz was attacked by his two neighbors and sought safety by appealing to Tiglath-Pileser III for assistance. The Great King of Assyria was only too willing, at the price of a heavy tribute, to come to the rescue of the kingdom of Jerusalem, capturing Damascus together with the king of Syria.

Over thirty years later, on the death of Sargon II (705), Hezekiah made an attempt to shake off the Assyrian yoke. Sennacherib (705-681) was occupied in the eastern part of his kingdom and could take no immediate action. In 701 he invaded Syria and Palestine, determined to carry the war down into Egypt. He was only prevented from destroying Jerusalem by the destruction of his army in the eastern Nile delta, but he was able to impose harsh terms of submission of Hezekiah, and Judah continued to live in a state of vassellage until her final fall a century later.

A.—THE MAJESTY OF YAHVEH THE KING

When contemplating the ruin of Samaria in his prophetic vision, Hosea had heard the complaint of a great unrequited love and the avenging cry of the deceived Spouse.

What especially strikes Isaiah in the same circumstances is the *majesty* and *holiness* of Yahveh the King. This was to be the particular intuition of the son of Amos, whose sight remained forever dazzled by the splendor of the vision at the outset of his prophetic career:

In the year King Uzziah died,
I saw the Lord Yahveh seated on a high and lofty throne,
with the train of his garment filling the temple. (6, 1)

That day—it was in the year 740—the young aristocrat of twenty-five was in the Temple, probably assisting officially in the "debir" facing the Holy of Holies at a solemn liturgical ceremony. It may also be assumed from his mentioning the death of Uzziah and his use of the title of King—usually avoided by the prophets—that the kingship of Yahveh was being once more proclaimed in the presence of the Ark that had been brought back to Jerusalem in triumph by David. Perhaps during the ceremony the prophet was thinking of the difficult times that seemed to be lying ahead for the kingdom of Judah.

All of a sudden the words of the liturgy revealed an un-suspected depth of meaning to him and opened up a hitherto unexplored field of human knowledge:

"Holy, holy, holy is Yahveh of hosts!
All the earth is filled with his glory. (6, 3)

While around him continued the hymns in praise of the glory of Yahveh the King, this same Lord of Hosts appeared visibly to him. For then on Isaiah was a changed man. His life took a new turn, and neither human disaster nor the events of history could appear to him under the same light. The vision was to alter his outlook so completely that, far from being disturbed at the storm clouds gathering in the East, he seems to be a calm observer standing on the sunlit mountain top to which he has suddenly been carried. With Yahveh he could say:

I will quietly look on from where I dwell. (18, 4)

☼   ☼   ☼

What was it, then, that Isaiah saw?

Amos, coming from Zion, had heard nothing but the rum-bling that heralded the distant storm, Hosea the sorrowing com-plaint of a forgotten Father and the angry protest of an outraged lover. Isaiah sees rather than hears. Before his eyes rises the image of Yahveh, *King*, awe-inspiring in His hieratic dignity, and supreme *Judge* standing at His tribunal:

Yahveh rises to accuse,
standing to try his people. (3, 13)

For the sin of Israel and of the world has reached its height:

For all this, his wrath is not turned back,
his hand is still outstretched. (9, 16 and 20; 10, 4)

3

It is the terrible God of Sinai who reappears in storm and lightning:

Yahveh will make his glorious voice heard,
and let it be seen how his arm descends
in raging fury and flame of consuming fire,
in driving storm and hail. (30, 30)

Before this almighty power giant trees are uprooted, mountains tremble on their foundations, nothing can stand up-right. How would the ridiculous fortifications built by the hand of man fare any better? What paltry human work of grandeur would still have any importance? What human gaze could meet that of the Lord of Hosts?

The haughty eyes of man will be lowered,
the arrogance of men will be abased,
and Yahveh alone will be exalted on that day. (2, 11 & 17)

Conscious of his nothingness, there will be nothing left to man on the Day of Wrath but to hide himself underground like a hunted beast fleeing to its lair:

Get behind the rocks,
hide in the dust,
from the terror of Yahveh
and the splendor of his majesty,
when he arises
to overawe the earth. (2, 10, 21)

✿   ✿   ✿

The crime most abhorrent to Yahveh is *pride*. As King he commands, but Israel refuses him obedience. As Judge he condemns, but Israel obstinately refuses to yield:

This is a rebellious people,
deceitful children,
children who refuse to obey
the law of Yahveh. (30, 9)

Under the blows that fall on them, these unnatural children ought to understand the lesson from experience and recognize the hand that strikes them, but instead their only thought is to rebuild the ruins without giving up the sins which caused them:

They said in arrogance and pride of heart,
"Bricks have fallen, but we will build with cut stone;
sycamores are felled, but we will replace them with cedars."
(9, 9-10)

That is why Yahveh will never have compassion on the proud city of Samaria. It glitters like a diadem in the midst of its valleys, but it will fade like a garland with which the guest at a banquet adorns himself:

The majestic garland of the drunkards of Ephraim
shall be trodden under foot,
and the fading flower of his glorious beauty. (28, 3-4)

But neither shall Judah escape punishment, because of the greed and corruption, the pride and arrogance of her nobles. Woe to the insatiable landowners who take up every inch of ground! (5, 8); woe to the fools who are wise in their own sight! (5, 21); woe to those who make wicked laws (10, 1) and the judges who take bribes to free the guilty! (5, 23); woe to those who pass their days in drunken revelry (5, 11-12). Woe to them all,

for they have spurned the law of Yahveh Sabaoth,
and scorned the word of the Holy One of Israel. (5, 24)

Woe also to the women of Jerusalem who parade their shameless arrogance in the streets of the holy city; they will become a prey to the lust of invading armies:

Yahveh said: "Because the daughters of Zion are haughty,
and walk with necks outstretched,
ogling and mincing as they go,
their anklets tinkling with every step,
the Lord shall cover the scalps of Zion's daughters with scabs,
and lay bare their nakedness." (3, 16-17)

✿   ✿   ✿

The God of Israel cannot permit man — and least of all his own people — to dare lift his impudent face at him. The aristocratic prophet feels intensely both the ridiculousness of human pride and the ironic compassion of the God of majesty who need only let fall his irresistible arm to crush and annihilate. Like a hunter with his hounds, Yahveh the King will whistle to call the flies from the rivers of Egypt and they will rise in clouds from the swamps, and hornets from the land of Assyria:

On that day Yahveh shall whistle for the fly
that is in the farthest streams of Egypt,
and for the bee in the land of Assyria.
All of them shall come and settle in the steep ravines
and in the rocky clefts,
on all thornbushes and on all pastures. (7, 18-19)

He will leave nothing undone to punish his deceitful children:

Yahveh raises up their foes against them
and stirs up their enemies to action:
Aram on the east and the Philistines on the west
devour Israel with open mouth. (9, 10-11)

But the deadliest weapon he has chosen and will wield in his mighty hand — not as a noble, gleaming sword but as a base cudgel fit for the contemptible backs of those it will belabor — is Assyria:

He will give a signal to a far-off nation,
and whistle to them from the ends of the earth;
speedily and promptly will they come.
None of them will stumble with weariness,
none will slumber and none will sleep.
None will have his waist belt loose,
nor the thong of his sandal broken. (5, 26-27)

Isaiah is alone in seeing that these unleashed hordes of men are unwittingly obeying the will of an invisible strategist, the God enthroned in Zion. It is by his command that the formidable Assyrian war machine has been set going. In stirring words the prophet describes its irresistible advance; like a tidal wave sweeping all before it the enemy host will flood, lay waste and submerge Israel (10, 27-34). But Assyria need not harbor any illusions about the significance of her short-lived triumph or take pride in it. When her usefulness as a weapon is finished, she will be broken in pieces:

Woe to Assyria!
My rod in anger, my staff in wrath! (10, 5)

for the pride of Assyria is more abominable to Him than the pride of Israel. Her's is not the rebellion of a son but the arrogance of a servant:

Will the axe boast against him who hews with it?
Will the saw exalt itself above him who wields it?
As if a rod could sway him who lifts it,
or a staff him who is not wood! (10, 15)

Isaiah is quite unimpressed by the vainglory of famous conquerors. Yahveh will soon make it vanish into thin air, and his prophet has only contempt and sarcasm for it. When, bloated with success, Sennacherib dares to boast before Jerusalem:

"By my own power I have done it,
and by my wisdom, for I am shrewd.
I have moved the boundaries of peoples;
their treasures I have pillaged,
and like a giant I have put down the enthroned.
My hand has seized like a nest the riches of nations;
as one takes eggs left alone, so I took in all the earth;
no one fluttered a wing, or opened a mouth, or chirped.
(10, 13-14)

Yahveh will answer his impudence with a judgment against which there is no appeal:

Because of your rage against me,
and your insolence which has reached my ears,
I will put my hook in your nose
and my bit in your mouth,
and make you return the way you came. (37, 29)

A lion irritated by a fly may get into a rage, but the God of Israel is not even annoyed when men become a nuisance. He has only to make an imperceptible gesture to chase them away or crush them. In any case, what will become of these haughty human great ones? When Sargon II comes to die and the world still goes on living, the inhabitants of Sheol will crowd round to see the late monarch arrive and will humble his ridiculous pride with words of gloomy irony:

You too have become weak like us,
you are the same as we are.

Down to the nether world your pomp is brought
with the music of your harps.
The couch beneath you is the maggot,
your covering the worm. (14, 10-11)

The Assyrian armies may well make the earth tremble and
sow panic everywhere, but all their vain tumult will not alter
the serenity of a mind imbued with the consciousness of God's
majesty. All the boasting and bragging of these conquerors of
a day is nothing but the idle chatter of impotent slaves. The
man whose gaze is fixed on Yahveh's throne can judge history
without letting himself be daunted by fear of its reverses; a
tidal wave is only a ripple on the sea's surface in his eyes. After
Yahveh has grasped hold of him Isaiah can no longer fear what
the rest of men fear; nothing, with the exception of God's vengeance, can ever be such as to make him afraid (8, 11-13).

For her part, Israel has no cause to be over-confident in the
thought that she is under the protection of a God whose majesty mocks at all human greatness. No one, least of all the
chosen people, can escape the all-seeing eye of Yahveh:

Woe to those who would hide their plans
too deep for Yahveh!
Who work in the dark, saying,
"Who sees us, or who knows us?" (29, 15)

If in the day of his vengeance, Yahveh has taken Assyria
for a rod, what does it matter what he will do with her afterwards? A rod is nothing but a rod, but Israel is the work of his
hands, like a vessel from the hands of the potter:

What perversity!
Shall the potter be taken to be the clay?
Shall what is made say of him who made it,
"He made me not!"

Or the vessel say of the potter,
"He does not understand!" (29, 16)

If he thinks it imperfect, is not the potter free to break it and begin again?

Yahveh shall hurl you down headlong, mortal man!
He shall grip you firmly and roll you up
and toss you like a ball into an open land
to perish there. (22, 17-18)

Never since the encounter on Sinai had Yahveh's unapproachable greatness been so intensely felt. While the mountain was then shaken by the violence of the tempest, Yahveh had revealed himself to his people as a force that nothing could withstand. Now that Israel was settled in the Promised Land and her very existence threatened, Yahveh the King shows himself again in all his power to his prophet. The chosen people must understand that if they wish to live they must humble their pride before the only Majesty that does not pass away and is able to make the whole world tremble:

With the Lord of hosts make your alliance
for him be your fear and your awe. (8, 13)

B.—HOLINESS AND CONSCIOUSNESS OF SIN

Affirmation of God leads naturally to man's need of a rule of morality. All fresh intuition of the mystery of God makes man more sensible to God's demands on him. As a corollary to this it can be asserted that the perception of the divine reality shows up by contrast with the reality of sin and that, the more eternal perfection is perceived, the more apparent becomes the notion of sin.

This law, standing out clearly in the Revelation of the Bible, has evidently failed to be recognized by Islam. While proclaiming the immutable oneness of the divinity, Mahomet does not appear to have had any intention of changing the hearts of believers. His message dissociated the problem of God from man's and just ignored it. Apart from belief, the Koran lays down only the rudimentary precept of the practice of a number of good works. The God of the Bible, on the other hand, is the more demanding the more he reveals himself, and the devout Israelite is obliged to try and resemble his God as far as he is able. The exhortation "Be holy, because I am holy" (Lev. 17, 26) is the theme inspired by the message of Isaiah which recurs insistently in the Code of Holiness. The Old Testament thus gradually prepares the ideal of perfection required by man's contact with God's holiness, which was to reach its fullness in the word's incarnation.

The revelation of God's holiness, which explains the whole history of Israel, also allowed each prophet to form a judgment on the conduct of the chosen people. The Bible, in fact, never attempts to give a rational justification of the moral prescriptions that it states. It is only through the knowledge of God that he finds in it that man discovers the motives of action, and the conscience of Israel is shaped and refined by a development of the idea of their relations with Yahveh.

When the prophets make their indictment of the chosen people, they base it on the same facts, judged in relation to God's perfection, but each of them colors his accusations to suit the sense of his particular message. Thus Amos is led to pinpoint their sin in the violation of the social prescriptions of the Covenant. Yahveh's love for his people allows Hosea to see it as a sin of ingratitude. It is God's glory that makes Isaiah aware of his own uncleanness and the defilement of his people:

Then I said, "Woe is me, I am doomed!
For I am a man of unclean lips,
living among a people of unclean lips;
yet my eyes have seen the King, the Lord of Hosts." (6, 5)

It was inevitable that this uncleanness should offend an eye that had been dazzled by the holiness of Yahveh the King:

Your silver is turned to dross,
your wine is mixed with water. (1, 22)

The undeniable evidence of this impurity leads Isaiah to compare it to the dross that has to be removed from a precious metal. God's holiness demands that Israel should live for him alone, and any sharing of her fidelity, any turning aside from it, is like a foreign body marring its purity.

Isaiah's thought, it can be seen, approximates that of Hosea, but the angle of vision is not the same. The prostitute theme, for instance, of which both of them make use, shows the difference of their approach. In the harlot Hosea sees a profanation of love while Isaiah sees the uncleanness:

How has she turned harlot, the faithful city,
so upright!
Justice used to lodge within her, but now,
murderers. (1, 21)

This idea of uncleanness in Isaiah needs further examination. In primitive times the term unclean was applied to creatures and objects believed to have a baleful influence, thereby causing an almost instinctive repulsion. A corpse was unclean because the dead man's spirit pursued the living while his body remained unburied and could be profaned. Blood that had been shed was unclean, because it cried for vengeance until the earth had covered it. It was this blood that came to symbolize all that was abhorrent, and particularly sin. Whereas we speak of the blackness of sin, ancient peoples—Egypt among others—saw it as the color of freshly shed blood:

Though your sins be like scarlet,
they may become white as snow;

though they be crimson red,
they may become white as wool. (1, 18)

Sin, of course, in early times *meant* only the breaking of social
or ritual taboos. It was not till later that it acquired a purer and
higher religious meaning when—as in Israel—it was applied to
the inobservance of prescriptions of the moral order. Even then,
the idea of sin retained something of its original sense, and in
describing it recourse was still made to the terms and modes
formerly used in the case of ritual impurity. Thus the prophet
could exclaim bitterly:

He looked for judgment, but see, bloodshed! (5,7)

Here the word bloodshed still gives the same impression of
horror as was caused by ritual impurity, but superimposed on
it there is also the sense of moral transgression, in particular the
violation of the laws of social justice already condemned by
Amos. This is still more noticeable in the vigorous apostrophe
in the first chapter of Isaiah:

Your hands are full of blood!
Wash yourselves clean!
Put away your misdeeds from before my eyes;
cease doing evil;
learn to do good.
Make justice your aim:
redress the wronged,
hear the orphan's plea,
defend the widow. (1, 15-17)

Israel's moral uncleanness produces in Isaiah the ancient
feeling of repulsion. Disgust, too, is the dominant note in his
description of Yahveh's rejection of the sacrifices by which
Israel with bloodstained hands thinks to honor Him:

What care I for the number of your sacrifices?
I have had enough of whole-burnt rams and fat of fatlings;
In the blood of calves, lambs and goats I find no pleasure.
When you come in to visit me, who asks these things of you?
Trample my courts no more!
Bring no more worthless offerings;
your incense is loathsome to me.
New moon and sabbath, calling of assemblies:
these I cannot bear.
Your new moons and festivals I detest;
they weigh me down, I tire of the load.
When you spread out your hands, I close my eyes to you;
though you pray the more, I will not listen.
Your hands are full of blood! (1, 11-15).

While Amos ends his message with a plea for obedience, and Hosea proclaims the need to learn the lesson of destitution from the desert, Isaiah prescribes only one remedy for Israel's uncleanness: Wash yourselves clean! (1, 16).

C.—CLEANSING BY FIRE

When Isaiah, overawed at the sight of Yahveh's holiness, groans at feeling himself "a man of unclean lips" (6, 5), one of the seraphim above the throne flies towards his to sanctify the lips which are to utter the divine message. Touching them with a burning coal he has taken from the altar with the ritual tongs, he removes the uncleanness from them:

"See, now that this has touched your lips,
your wickedness is removed,
your sin is purged." (6, 7)

The germ of all Isaiah's teaching lies here: only the cleansing fire can re-establish communion between the sinner and God's holiness like metal, man can be purified only by being tried in the furnace:

I will turn my hand against you,
and refine your dross in the furnace,
removing all your alloy. (1, 25)

It can be noted, by the way, that fire accompanies Yahveh's appearances just as lightning flashes out from the storm. The seraphim that Isaiah sees around Yahveh's throne are, by the etymology of the word itself, associated with the idea of burning, and there is also a burning in the sting of a snakebite. It is noticeable that in the *ureus* of the Pharaoh's crown, the snake and the flame are found together.

But the flame which elsewhere—in Amos for example—is an instrument of destruction, in Isaiah is essentially an agent of purification. And if it purifies, it is in order to save:

The Light of Israel will become a fire,
Israel's Holy One a flame,
that burns and consumes his briers
and his thorns in a single day. (10, 17)

Yahveh's avenging fire, while destroying the brushwood, leaves the tall trees in full view:

The remnant of the trees in his forest will be so few that a child may count them. (10, 19)

The storm whose approach was announced by Amos spares nothing on its way; the destruction foretold by Isaiah in other figures of speech is almost equally complete:

From the sole of the foot to the head
there is no sound spot. (1, 6)

On that day the Lord shall shave
with the razor hired from across the River. (7, 20)

But something will remain, even if it is very little:

... you shall flee,
until you are left as a flagstaff on the mountaintop,
as a flag on the hill. (30, 17)

The imagery may change but the idea remains the same. The Assyrian flood will sweep over Judah but her head will remain above water (8, 6-8). The vineyard will be laid waste and covered with briers and thorns (5, 5-6) but the hut in it will remain standing. Otherwise, the prophet adds:

Unless the Lord of hosts had left us a scanty remnant,
we had become as Sodom,
We should be like Gomorrah. (1, 9)

even though it will be a very small one:

Your voice shall be a ghost's from the earth,
and your words like chirping from the dust. (29, 4)

But—and this is the important point—all the same there will be a remnant, and in spite of the range of the punishment, it will confirm the lastingness of the Promise. What is striking here is the twofold character of Isaiah's intuition: while confirming the message of condemnation announced by his predecessors, the prophet is emphatic in announcing the realization of the high hopes founded on the word of Yahveh.

Though the storm of fire may break over the people of God, it does not prevent Isaiah from contemplating the kingship of Yahveh, who as from an inaccessible peak dominates all human events. But to proclaim the kingship of the national God was, as we know, the same as affirming the stability of his reign. If Amos refused to become the herald of this kingship, it was because he was addressing Israel, and Samaria might have been too easily reassured if the thought of Yahveh the King had overshadowed the threat of death that lay on her. But Isaiah's words are directed at Judah, and so there is no reason for him to feel the same reluctance. The line of David had received the firm promises of the Covenant, and so even while the flames were about to sweep across the kingdom, the prophet could evoke the image of Yahveh the King enthroned above Jerusalem, and recall the immunity that his city, its temple and royal dynasty would continue to enjoy.

The oracle of Emmanuel, connected with the episode of Ahaz, and that of the future of the Holy City, are a perfect illustration of the double aspect of Isaiah's message. On the one hand he confirms the perpetuity of David's house and the inviolability of Jerusalem; on the other hand he announces the disasters that are about to befall the monarchy and the city, in order both to destroy them and to save them by purification.

          ✿   ✿   ✿

The monarchical system in ancient East was founded on the kingship of the national god. It was to the god-king that in a critical situation the monarch sacrificed his first-born to save the dynasty. The king of Moab, for example, had submitted to this rite when Jehoram of Israel and Jehoshaphat of Judah threatened his capital, and was convinced that Chemosh, the Moabite god, caused them to raise the siege (2 Kings, 3, 27). The Book of Kings also relates how Ahaz sacrificed his first-born, but there is no mention of the time or the circumstances. It would be natural, however, to refer this sacrifice to the only time during his reign when Ahaz was himself in danger. This was when Rezin of

Damascus aided by Pekah of Samaria was marching against Jerusalem with the intention of setting a king of his own upon the throne, and

> the heart of the king and the heart of the people trembled as the trees of the forest tremble in the wind. (7, 2)

If this hypothesis is true, it would probably be on his return from Tophet where he had sacrificed his son that the king saw the prophet coming towards him. We know that Isaiah had been ordered by Yahveh to go to meet Ahaz:

> Then Yahveh said to Isaiah:
> Go out to meet Ahaz, you and your son Shear-Jashub,
> at the end of the conduit of the upper pool,
> on the highway of the fuller's field. (7, 3)

It is difficult to believe that the time and place chosen by Yahveh were fortuitous, or that the king found himself in the valley to the south of the city—on the royal road, be it noted, that led up to Zion—for the simple purpose of inspecting the fortifications. If, as may be thought, Ahaz was taking part in a solemn religious ceremony and the prophet found him when the procession was starting off, then the meeting in that place and in those circumstances has a much greater dramatic significance. It must be admitted, however, that the connection between the sacrifice of the heir to the throne and the Emmanuel prophecy encounters a difficulty. Why did not the prophet of purity inveigh against the barbarous rite which condemned the first-born to the flames when, a little later, Jeremiah has no hesitation whatever in violently condemning the monstrous practice?

It may be said in reply that Isaiah nowhere makes any allusion to the practice, as if the time had not yet come to pronounce upon it. At the same time the general tenor of his message was such that we may safely say the prophet saw in this human sacrifice especially a crime against faith: there was no need for the king to sacrifice his first-born in order to ensure that Yahveh would be faithful to His promises. Heaven and earth had been witnesses to the covenant made with David, and as if this covenant itself were not enough, Yahveh was ready to confirm it with a sign like the rainbow after the deluge. By the mouth of his prophet He says to Ahaz:

> Ask for a sign from Yahveh, your God:
> let it be deep as the nether world,
> or high as the sky. (7, 3)

He offers Ahaz this sign to help him believe in His word, for ultimately this is what He requires of him. But Ahaz refuses to believe and prefers to rely on the magic effect of the sacrifice. Hypocritically he is ready to hide his lack of faith under a pious pretext:

> But Ahaz answered, "I will not ask!
> I will not tempt Yahveh!" (7, 12)

In spite of the king's obstinacy, however, God will not go back on His word. The impiety of one man will not prevent Him from remembering David, whose name is the only one mentioned:

> Listen, O house of David! . . .
> the Lord himself will give you this sign:
> the virgin shall be with child,
> and bear a son,
> and shall name him Emmanuel. (7, 13-14)

The dynasty will continue according to the promise. The father's part in this birth is intentionally passed over in silence. The initiative belongs to God alone, God who "opens the womb" and whose son the future king will be. The princess—she only is spoken of—will call him Emmanuel, "God with us." The name will express at the same time the anguished appeal of Judah whose only recourse is to Yahveh: "God *be* with us," and the faith that was wanting in Ahaz: "God *is* with us."

Such is the reassuring side of the prophecy, but the child who is to be king "shall live on curds and honey" (7, 15). This food of paradise that is given in Deuteronomy as the ideal nourishment in the Promised Land will be forced on him by the tragic circumstances of there being nothing else to eat, when everyone will have to be satisfied with the little that is left (7, 21-22). The events that will accompany this happy birth are announced in the gloomiest terms:

> Before the child learns to reject the bad
> and choose the good,
> the land of those two kings whom you dread
> shall be deserted.
> Yahveh shall bring upon you and upon your people
> and your father's house
> days worse than any since Ephraim seceded from Judah.
>
> (7, 16-17)

Tradition has insisted especially on the first part of the prophecy, the birth of the Messiah, but the attendant circumstances should not be overlooked. The prophecy is perhaps more concerned to stress the virgin's sufferings than her virginal conception— "thy own soul a sword shall pierce" (Luke 2, 35).

The Presence of Shear-Jashub with his father brings us back to the theme of the small remnant: the axe will fell the tree of Jesse, but a branch will grow from the stump:

> A shoot shall sprout from the stump of Jesse,
> and from his roots a bud shall blossom. (11, 1)

The twofold aspect of Isaiah's intuition is found again in the theme of the inviolability of Yahveh's City. Before the invasion of Sennacherib the prophet had declared that the enemy would not be able to lay a hand on Jerusalem, which would be safeguarded by the presence of the thrice-holy God:

Yahveh has established Zion,
and in her the afflicted of his people will find refuge. (14, 32)

While Hosea saw the only chance of rebirth for Israel in a return to her desert origins, Isaiah, in whom the prophet and the courtier are one, thinks primarily of a restoration of the glorious city of David:

I will restore your judges as at first,
and your counselors as in the beginning;
after that you shall be called the city of justice, faithful city.
(1, 26)

The restoration, however, presupposes a purification which will be one of fire, from which Yahveh dwelling on Mount Zion will not spare his city, for he "has a fire in Zion and a furnace in Jerusalem" (31, 9).

The Holy City, like Emmanuel, is given a name with a double meaning: *Ariel,* "hearth of God." Thus Jerusalem will be both protected and purified by fire. The hopes sustained by the New Year liturgy are thus once more accompanied by the direst prophecies of woe:

Woe to Ariel, Ariel,
the city where David encamped!
Add year to year,
let the feasts come round.
But I will bring distress upon Ariel,
with mourning and grief.

You shall be to me like Ariel,
I will encamp like David against you;
I will encircle you with outposts
and set up siege works against you.
Prostrate you shall speak from the earth,
and from the base dust your words shall come. (29, 1-4)

✿   ✿   ✿

Isaiah is not the prophet of a serene messianic message as he is often depicted. He is constantly haunted by the thought of the cleansing fire from the day when he first experienced it in himself. The twofold aspect of his message, in which threat is joined to promise, finds a long and powerful echo in the whole economy of salvation. The hand of God laid upon man leads him to salvation through the flame that consumes his impurities; and like Christ who was to be a sign of contradiction, the Rock of Israel rises like a stumbling block:

He shall be a snare, an obstacle and a stumbling stone
to both the houses of Israel,
a trap and a snare to those who dwell in Jerusalem;
and many among them shall stumble and fall,
broken, snared and captured. (8, 14-15)

D.—THE CONCLUSION ON THE HOLY MOUNTAIN

Amid the clash of empires shaking the world and threatening to wipe Israel off the map, Yahveh the King is the only one refuge left to her, but to gain that refuge she must pass through the flame. Yahveh does not guarantee his people endless possession of their land as an automatic certainty. They can live in it only in so far as his sovereign will allows, on condition that the stiff-necked people accept the necessary purification and genuinely become his people. Unlike the gods of other nations, he is quite unmoved by the idle incantations of a worship copy-

ing that of Baal. After their settlement in Canaan, the beliefs of
Israel had been largely influenced by the surrounding nature
worship with its religion based on the cyclic recurrence of the
forces of nature. Under the prophets' influence especially that of
Isaiah, a new and original hope was to guide their uncertain
steps towards a clearer goal: they would live in the expectation
of a unique and decisive event which would bring them forever
to a state of peace and plenty.

Thus Israel becomes aware that her history implies an evolution. After its beginning on Sinai it was progressing towards a
goal, the way God had traced out to her.

*   *   *

How was it, we may ask, the prophet was led to bring about
what was nothing less than a revolution in Israel's thought?

The new theme of the final battle on the holy mountain,
which was to have such outstanding importance and become one
of the major themes of apocalyptic writing, was probably inspired by an historic event fraught with grave consequences for
Judah—Sennacherib's offensive against Jerusalem in 701, which
put her faith in the invulnerability of Zion to the crucial test.

Isaiah sees from afar the terrible threat of the Assyrian conqueror seemingly able to inflict the same fate on Jerusalem as
had befallen Samaria:

Just as my hand reached out to idolatrous kingdoms
that had more images than Jerusalem and Samaria,
just as I treated Samaria and her idols,
shall I not do to Jerusalem and her graven images? (10, 10-11)

The threat does not take long to become a reality. Sennacherib stands before Yahveh's city, ready to hurl the might of
his endless host against its ramparts:

Ah! the roaring of many peoples
that roar like the roar of the seas!
The surging of nations that surge
like the surging of mighty waves! (17, 12)

Those who had placed reliance in the belief that the holy city
was inviolable are scandalized, but Isaiah is not in the least
perturbed. The vision that had inaugurated his prophetic
mission had raised him to a higher plane where he shares in God's
imperturbable serenity (18, 4). He knows that Yahveh the
King who sees the ebb and flow of all human events is also he
who regulates them, and will intervene at the moment he has
decided:

As a lion or a lion cub
growling over its prey,
with a band of shepherds
assembled against it,
is neither frightened by their shouts
nor disturbed by their noise,
so shall the Lord of hosts come down to wage war
upon the mountain and hill of Zion. (31, 4)

Then at the hour when hope is reborn, when voices are lifted
up in morning prayer and the priests of Egypt awake their sleeping gods with their incantations, the panic of the day before will
give place to the joyfulness of victory:

God shall rebuke them,
and they shall flee far away;
windswept, like chaff on the mountains,
like tumbleweed in a storm?
In the evening they spread terror,
before morning they are gone! (17, 13-14)

In this there is nothing comparable to the ephemeral successes of the gods of the gentiles who are supposed to defend their country when it is threatened, but are at the mercy of events over which they have no control. The God of Israel is not the Lord of a piece of land but of a people and the whole of its history, the same God as the Yahveh of the Covenant. As he came down on Sinai in storm and lightning, so he will come to visit Zion;

with thunder, earthquake and great noise,
whirlwind, storm, and the flame of consuming fire. (29, 6)

In his tremendous epiphany he will subdue his enemies:

See the name of Yahveh coming from afar
in burning wrath, with lowering
his tongue is like a consuming fire;
his breath, like a flood in a ravine
that reaches suddenly to the neck,
He will winnow the nations with a destructive winnowing,
and put a bridle on the jaws of the peoples. (30, 27-28)

His outstretched arm will be much more than a reminder of the victorious arm that struck the waters of the Red Sea to open a passage for the Hebrews; it is the same arm working for the realization of the same design. The joyful chants that will follow the Assyrian retreat will re-echo those at the celebration of the Pasch commemorating the rout of Pharaoh's army:

You will sing as on a night when a feast is observed,
and be merry of heart as one marching along with a flute
toward the mountain of Yahveh, toward the Rock of Israel,
accompanied by the timbrels and lyres. (30, 29)

This is the direction taken by the religious reform of Hezekiah, who thereby shows himself to be a king after the prophet's own heart. By associating the thought of Judah's salvation through the intervention of Yahveh with Israel's deliverance from Egypt, he was probably trying to restore the feast of the Passover to its full significance. The title of Baal would never again be referred to Yahveh; only Yahveh the King would remain. And this kingship, which both Amos and Hosea pass over in silence, regains all its prestige in Isaiah by his integrating it so perfectly into the scheme of the Covenant.

No other nation of the ancient world had been able (in the nature of things it was, of course, impossible) to establish a relation between the power attributed to its sedentary god and the course of its history. Israel alone had become aware of the unique phenomenon that Isaiah was preaching: the everyday God, the God who gives the harvests, was the same God of Sinai. But this discovery was still only fragmentary and required further analysis. The kingship of Yahveh as revealed by Isaiah had a feature that had not been previously noted. It was not, as was thought, a kingship existing in the present and confined to a limited territory, like that of a Baal; its full development among men was to come in the future, as a result of a series of divine interventions unique in human history.

This does not mean that the development was not proceeding in the present. The preparation had begun from the first day of the Covenant. The long work was proceeding by stages, appearing to be gathering momentum the more it progressed and the coming of Yahveh approached, like a stone detached from the mountain side and rolling down with ever increasing speed till it comes to rest in the valley below. The comparison is not quite apt with regard to the kingship of Yahveh, for its course was an upward movement. The last of its stages, the one that would set a seal on the adventure that had lasted almost a thousand years, would be the final victory that Yahveh would win on the holy mountain.

While hitherto good and evil had contended with results as

short-lived as the mythological struggles between Horus and
Set, Ra and Apopi, Baal and Môt, Isaiah announces the inevitable
defeat of darkness by light, of affliction by joy, and of war by
peace:

> The people who walked in darkness
> have seen a great light;
> upon those who dwelt in the land of gloom
> a light has shown.
> You have brought them abundant joy
> and great rejoicing. . . .
> For the yoke that burdened them,
> the pole on their shoulder,
> and the rod of their taskmaster
> you have smashed, as on the day of Midian.
> For every boot that tramped in battle,
> every cloak rolled in blood,
> will be burned as fuel for flames. . . .
> His dominion is vast and forever peaceful. (9, 1-6)

Isaiah sees this final intervention of God as imminent and
apparently identifies it with the retreat of the Assyrian armies,
in which, if any prefiguration was intended, it could only be a
very approximate one. This success, purely relative and of questionable importance, was shown within a century to have been
only a breathing space for Judah before the unprecedented
disaster of her destruction. But the fact hardly matters—a mountain spur may be mistaken by a climber for the summit it is
hiding, but the summit is still there. It cannot be said that Isaiah
did not contemplate the final battle, even though he may have
mistaken it for an episode in sacred history.

After the decisive struggle there will be a new era, the
ultimate one. From then on the Prince with the wonderful names
(9, 5) will reign over a liberated Zion. The rod from the root
of Jesse, upon which the spirit of Yahveh rests, will slay the

wicked with the breath of his lips (11, 4). All nature, which
every spring feels its numbed forces reawakening and re-adorns
itself, will be profoundly changed. It will be like a new creation
issuing from the hands of the Creator, unsullied by bloodshed. Carnivorous animals will feed on grass as before the
Deluge (11, 7); wild beasts will cease to devour each other and
none shall do harm to man (11, 8). Universal harmony, the
dream of all civilizations, will be established lovelier and more
perfect than at the beginning of time. And peace, the greatest
and most desirable of all the benefits granted to creatures, will
reblossom for ever under the eyes of Yahveh:

> There shall be no harm or ruin
> on all my holy mountain;
> for the earth shall be filled with knowledge of Yahveh,
> as the water covers the sea. (11, 9)

* * *

The messianic nature of Isaiah's message had a profound effect
upon Israel and changed its outlook in two ways in particular.
There is no longer any question of a periodical return, a going
round in a circle, to which mankind seemed condemned like a
squirrel in a cage. Instead there is a continuous movement starting from a point and progressing towards a goal that can be
perceived. Cyclic hopes are replaced by a linear hope, the
mediocrity and limitation of purely human wait by the breadth
and magnificence of a divinely inspired certitude.

Preceded by a column of cloud or of fire and following a
route which, though mysterious and complicated, was nevertheless to lead them unfailingly to Canaan, the land of serfs
from the land of Gessen had journeyed for forty years in the
desert—the time necessary for the generation to die out whose
hearts had hardened in the long sojourn in Egypt. Like them
Israel was now on the march, behind Yahveh the King, towards

the new Land of Promise. All their murmurings and revolts, all their impatience and trials, all their doubts and aspirations, all their golden calves and alternatings between faith and impiety, all that still remains for them to suffer and gain, all has been, is, and will be only stages which one after the other are left behind so that, after the decisive outcome of the final battle, they may reach the goal of their long pilgrimage.

In the second place, as long as the faith of Israel was more or less influenced by cyclic beliefs, Jerusalem was only the point on which her ambitions and hopes were centered. But now that the route she was unconsciously following is revealed, Jerusalem appears as a summit on which all is accomplished with the endless triumph of Yahveh the King.

The hope of the Messiah announced by the great prophet was to go on increasing with time. It would become purified but never be repudiated. The Day of Yahveh that Isaiah saw approaching would later be referred to the end of the world when the New Jerusalem would descend from above in splendor:

Behold the dwelling of God with men, and he will dwell with them. And they will be his people, and God himself will be with them as their God. . . . And he who was sitting on the throne said, "Behold, I make all things new." (Apocalypse 21, 3-5)

E.—FAITH THROUGH PURIFICATION AS THE WAY TO PEACE

Amos had seen death and destruction approaching on the road to perdition which Israel was obliviously treading. Isaiah sees a barrier of fire, but the flame will purify more than it consumes, and beyond it there is an endless stretch of refreshing coolness and security where Yahveh awaits his people. In her almost desperate wandering there is only one gesture that Israel has to make in order to escape unharmed from the fiery zone and enter the kingdom of peace:—"My people will live in peaceful country" (32, 18)—the gesture so simple and apparently easy of placing her sinful and impotent hand in the hand of her God. Even should everything around fall into ruin, if she abandons herself to this ungentle but paternal hand that sustains and guides her, Israel has nothing further to fear. What Yahveh requires and expects from her is faith:

> Unless your faith is firm
> you shall not be firm. (7, 9)

This faith was held fully by Isaiah from the very first moment of his vocation and nothing could ever shake it. When, on the approach of the two allied kings, the hearts of Ahaz and the people "trembled as the trees of the forest tremble in the wind" (7, 2), the prophet tried to communicate to Judah the serenity that his faith gave him:

> Take care you remain tranquil and do not fear;
> let not your courage fail! (7, 4)

For, after all, who were these enemies? Only Syria and Ephraim, Rezin and the "son of Remaliah," a usurper whom the prophet does not even deign to mention by name, the son of a nobody. But if one remembers that Jerusalem is Yahveh, it is ridiculous to get excited "because of these two smouldering stumps of firebrands" (7, 4). A few years later the city was to be threatened not by two petty kings but by Sennacherib. The danger was much more serious as the net tightened round Judah. Jerusalem was filled with apprehension, for this time the struggle was obviously quite unequal. How could they escape, or where could they find safety? The mighty Lord of Assyria, if we may believe the Assyrian chronicles, had made it a point of honor to capture Hezekiah and imprison him like a bird in a cage. Isaiah's faith was put to the hardest test but it was no more shaken than before. If Yahveh so willed, the caged bird would fly away and be out of reach and the haughty hand of the Assyrian would be left clutching at the empty air. Isaiah endeavors to make his countrymen share the strength of his assurance and in the name of Yahveh he repeats untiringly to the panic-striken people:

O my people, who dwell in Zion,
do not fear the Assyrian,
though he strikes you with a rod,
and raises his staff against you. (10, 24)

Judah has no reason to complain, for the faith that is asked of them does not require a superhuman effort or stoic virtue. To remain calm and serene like the prophet himself, it would be enough for them to judge the world and events not according to human standards but in the light of the God who rules the destiny of empires and decides the course of history. Let Israel keep her eyes fixed on the sovereign power of Yahveh the King and she will have no reason to fear anyone, except it be Yahveh himself.

With the Lord of hosts make your alliance—
for him be your fear and your awe. (8, 13)

To find the calm that strengthens against the strongest, to grasp the hand that guides unharmed through the greatest perils, to be armed with faith as with an invulnerable breastplate, it is first necessary to turn towards God and be converted.

By waiting and by calm you shall be saved,
in quiet and in trust your strength lies. (30, 15)

But this is precisely what Judah will not accept—"But this you did not wish" (30, 15)—and if she has not been able to remain faithful to the love of her God, how can she be capable of remembering him?

And so Ahaz, panic-stricken at the approach of Rezin and

Pekah, can find no other solution but to place himself under the protection of Assyria. This desperate act of diplomacy was to prove the source of irreparable disaster. Like the sorcerer's apprentice the king of Judah had started off a mechanism of destruction that could never be halted. Hosea had already noted "When they sow the wind they shall reap the whirlwind," and so

> because this people has rejected the waters of Shiloah
> that flow gently,
> and melts with fear befor the loftiness
> of Rezin and Remaliah's son,
> therefore the Lord raises against them the waters of the
>   River, great and mighty.
> It shall rise above all its channels,
> and overflow all its banks;
> it shall pass over Judah,
> and flood it all throughout. (8, 6-8)

Instead of returning to her God when she realizes the truth, Judah will obstinately and blindly continue to seek a way out of her difficulties by recourse to the vain expedients suggested by short-sighted human prudence, convinced that she is able to forge her own destiny:

> We have made a covenant with death,
> and with the nether world we have made a pact;
> when the overwhelming scourge passes,
> it will not reach us. (28, 15)

For, Isaiah ironically adds,

> we have made lies our refuge,
> and in falsehood we have found a hiding place. (ib.)

The illusion is a double one. First of all they think they can

rely on their own war potential. Jerusalem makes feverish preparations for the siege, strengthens her ramparts and repairs her
defenses:

> On that day you looked to the weapons
> in the House of the Forest;
> you saw that the breaches in the City of David
> were many;
> you collected the water of the lower pool.
> You numbered the houses of Jerusalem,
> tearing some down to strengthen the wall. (22, 8-10)

With the usual absurd enthusiasm that attends the beginning
of a war the population acclaims the troops marching past, while
amid their deafening cheers Isaiah cannot refrain from uttering
a discordant note at the thought of the disparity of Israel's forces
with those of Assyria:

> What is the matter with you now,
> that you have gone up,
> all of you, to the housetops,
> O city full of noise and chaos,
> O wanton town! (22, 1-2)

After this Judah becomes embroiled in power politics. She had
called in Assyria against Damascus and Samaria, and Assyria
had shown herself only too much interested in the affairs of the
countries on her western frontier. Now that her protector
threatens to annex her, she turns for help to Egypt.

Hezekiah might have remembered that the negotiations of
King Hoshea with Pharaoh had hastened Samaria's end, but now
the temptation has all the appearance of a move dictated by
political wisdom. The armies of the Egyptian empire to the
south had themselves offered to come to the rescue of Jerusalem.
They were the only ones capable of halting the invader; uneasily

watching the progress of Assyrian power, Pharaoh was feeling alarmed about the security of his own frontiers, and it was in his interest to maintain the independence of Judah as a buffer state. His ambassadors were everywhere doing their best to stir up revolt against Assyria and to form alliances.

What Hezekiah did not see was that Pharaoh's intention was less to support his new allies than to make use of them for his own purposes. He had already sacrificed them in advance as a means of wearing out the enemy and thus breaking the force of the blow which appeared inevitable. What escaped Hezekiah was self-evident to Isaiah. When he crudely calls Egypt "a people good for nothing" and "Rahab the idle" (30, 7) he is trying to show up the cynical wait-and-see policy she has adopted in the hope that time and the resistance of her allies will be to her advantage. So Judah is out of her mind to rely on any real help from Pharaoh, and, worse still, to drain her own resources in order to pay for the fancied support of a people doomed to destruction in their turn:

The Egyptians are men, not God,
their horses are flesh, not spirit. (31, 3)

To show his disapproval the prophet has recourse to a symbolic action. For three years he walks through Jerusalem "naked and barefoot" (20, 3) as a sign that

the king of Assyria shall lead away captives from Egypt,
    and exiles from Ethiopia,
young and old, naked and barefoot,
    with buttocks uncovered (the shame of Egypt). (20, 4)

Then Judah will be filled with confusion when she realizes her mistake, and will lament:

"Look at our hope! We have fled here for help and deliverance
from the King of Assyria; where can we flee now?" (20, 6)

Isaiah denounces the folly and danger of such expedients:

Woe to those who go down to Egypt for help,
who depend upon horses,
who put their trust in chariots because of their number
and in horsemen because of their combined power! (31, 1)

Yet it would be so simple to seek safety where it is really to be
found, in Yahveh, and in Yahveh alone. While they are busily
putting Jerusalem in a state of defense, Isaiah exclaims bitterly:

But you have not looked to the city's Maker,
nor have you considered him who built it long ago. (22, 11)

During discussions with Egypt he continues to deplore Israel's
obstinacy in setting her hopes on human alliances:

But they look not to the Holy One of Israel
nor seek Yahveh. (31, 1)

Isaiah would never have agreed with our dictum that Heaven
helps those who help themselves. Yahveh has once and for all
taken charge of the destinies of his people, so why should they
try to find collaborators for him? It is idle for Israel to claim
that she is furthering Yahveh's cause by acting thus. It is Yahveh
who defends his people, and not the people who defend their
God.

The one thing Yahveh expects from Israel is faith, which is
sufficient for everything. When all other help fails, let Israel
finally decide to entrust herself totally to her King Yahveh
Sabaoth, and God will manifest himself to her in the sight of
the whole world.

THE SERVANT OF YAHVEH AND THE
EIGHTH CENTURY PROPHETS

4 In ancient times there was no dissociation between the messenger and his message. The character of the one formed part of the nature of the other. Thus at the time of Absalom's rebellion, when David was sitting at the gates of the town waiting for news of the battle, the watchman saw in the distance a man running, and recognizing him as Ahimaaz, the son of Zadok, he informs the king who exclaims: "He is a good man, and comes with good news" (2 Sam. 18, 27). David also had ordered the execution of the Amalekite who announced the death of Saul to him joyfully. The punishment was not only for having laid his hand on the Lord's anointed but also for being the bearer of such a message—"He thought he brought good tidings; I apprehended and slew him, which was the reward I gave him for his news" (2 Sam. 4, 10). And the Sage says:

A wicked messenger brings on disaster;
but a trustworthy envoy is a healing remedy. (Prov. 13, 17)

The same applied to any of the prophets, who after all were only the messengers of God. A prophet to his hearers was the man of his message, the man of the Word. This idea must be kept in mind to understand the position that the prophet came to occupy in Israel, which was one both of great difficulty and great prestige.

Prophets were not something peculiar to the Jews. All civilizations have had interpreters of the thought and will of the gods —soothsayers, oracles, visionaries and seers who claimed to speak in their name. Before any important enterprise those in power were careful to consult the official spokesmen of the god and tried, naturally, to have a reply suited to what they wanted. If by chance the oracle lent itself to a double meaning, the more convenient one was chosen. If the meaning was beyond doubt, it might be accepted with resignation or rejected by the more violent or more authoritarian, and appeal made to another oracle. Even the most scrupulous sought a means of circumventing the gods, as if it were a battle of wits.

The attitude of some of the kings of Israel hardly seems inspired by a higher sense of religion than this. If the prophet announced some reversal, they did not hesitate to accuse him of ill will and even persecute him. Asa threw Hanani into prison (2 Chron. 16, 10); Jezebel threatened to kill Elijah, who saved his life only by flight (I Kings 19, 1-3); Ahab, determined to retake Ramoth from the Syrians, would have been content to accept the reassuring oracle of Zedekiah the son of Chenaanah (I Kings 22, 10-12), but on the advice of Jehoshaphat he sent for Micaiah the son of Imlah, who foretold disaster. The unfortunate prophet was thereupon beaten, thrown into prison and fed "with the bread of affliction" (I Kings 22, 17-28).

So it was that the kings always found some more prudent prophet who was ready to give only the answer that was expected. The prophet Micah was later to inveigh against them:

> Her prophets divine for money,
> while they rely on Yahveh, saying,
> "Is not Yahveh in the midst of us?
> No evil can come upon us!" (Micah 3, 11)

The genuine prophets of Israel were not distinguished, at least in appearance, from these charlatans. The outward form of their messages was, if not identical, at least analogous. But the content could not be the same. The pseudo-prophets make Yahveh speak, but with the true prophets it is Yahveh who speaks. The first say what they know is wanted; the others make known the will of Yahveh which, as often as not, is in direct contrast with the desires of the people. The originality of the prophets of Israel lies in this, that they never lower themselves to tone down their message or to invent it, as the prophets attached to the Court did. The hand of God, for them, cannot be forced. The "false" prophets, after all, were only practicing a profession which was all the more profitable according to the degree of skill and pliancy they showed.

The true prophet, on the other hand, had not chosen his mission himself. It had been imposed on him by God, often against his own will. His whole life and existence were pledged to a ministry which he could not refuse. If Hosea falls in love with Gomer, it is not because he feels the urge of a natural passion. His behavior is dictated by Yahveh himself, so that his love may serve for the lesson he wishes to teach Israel. His unconventional marriage was to be the symbol of Yahveh's love for his people in a land which "gives itself to harlotry" (Hosea 1, 2). Yahveh himself gives their names to the children born of this union, names which have a symbolic meaning of the judgment pronounced against Israel: *Jezreel* recalls the famous battle field; *Lo-Ruhama* is the "unloved"; *Lo-Ammi* is "not my people" (Hosea 1, 4-9).

Isaiah was to say in his turn:

Look at me and the children whom Yahveh has given me: we are signs and portents in Israel from Yahveh Sabaoth.
(Is. 8, 18)

One of his sons is named *Shear-Yashub*, "a remnant will re-

82

turn," while the name of the other, *Maher-Shalal-Hash-Baz*, fore-tells the imminent sack of Samaria and Damascus. The prophet himself, as has been seen, receives an order to walk naked and barefoot through the streets of Jerusalem for three years as "a sign and a portent" of what will happen to the men of Egypt and Kush (Is. 20, 3).

The prophet of Israel is thus heart and mouth, body and soul, the *interpreter* of the Word of Yahveh as it seeks to fashion the chosen people for the accomplishment of the great design as a collective experience. But from the very beginning Israel shows herself to be, if not hard of hearing—it was impossible not to hear the powerful voices of her God's heralds—at any rate hard of heart. Hosea alludes to this when he makes a contrast between one of the patriarchs and the first great prophet: on the one hand Jacob, calculating, astute and unscrupulous, whose lack of imagination and seriousness of purpose almost compromised the work of emancipation; Moses on the other, whose inflexible authority keeps Israel on the straight path of her destiny:

> When Jacob fled to the land of Aram,
> he served for a wife;
> for a wife Israel tended sheep.
> By a prophet Yahveh brought Israel out of Egypt,
> and by a prophet they were protected. (Hosea 12, 13-14)

The struggle was between Israel's obduracy, in which Jacob lived on, and the prophets continuing the work of Moses:

> I granted many visions
> and spoke to the prophets,
> through whom I set forth examples. (Hosea 12, 11)

The mercifulness of God's patient way of teaching his people is evident, but there was to be nothing weak or soft about it; it meant that their sins would be untiringly denounced.

But as for me, I am filled with power,
with authority and with might,
to declare to Jacob his crimes,
and to Israel his sins. (Micah 3, 8)

There will be no trace of indulgence in the condemnation
of Israel's obstinacy:

He shall remember their iniquity
and punish their sins. (Hosea 9, 9)

And there will be no appeal against their condemnation:

I smote them through the prophets,
I slew them by the words of my mouth. (Hosea 6, 5)

The more Yahveh shines his light, the more Israel sinks into
darkness; the more the word is preached, the more hardened
their hearts become. Almost as if with a sense of weariness Yahveh tells his prophet:

Go and say to this people:
Listen carefully, but you shall not understand!
Look intently, but you shall know nothing!
You are to make the heart of this people sluggish,
to dull their ears and close their eyes;
else their eyes will see, their ears hear,
their heart understand,
and they will turn and be healed. (Is. 6, 9-10)

Man and God seem to be living in two quite separate spheres
in which it is impossible for their thoughts to run along the
same lines. Israel is impervious to God's word; the reason is
simple and Isaiah gives it: the fundamental impurity of man

is incompatible with God's holiness, and as long as Israel refuses to be cleansed, she will remain deaf to the voice of the prophets. If anything, Israel is astonished at their language coming to disturb the calm of her infidelity. She finds it shocking and not to be tolerated:

> Let them not preach of these things!
> Shame shall not overtake us.
> Would the house of Jacob be cursed?
> Has Yahveh lost patience?
> Are such his deeds?
> Do not his words promise good for his people
> Israel? (Micah 2, 6-7)

Israel will not allow anyone to censure her. The prophet posing as a redresser of wrongs is a disturber of the peace, an undesirable who should be silenced:

> They say to the seers,
> "Have no visions";
> to the prophets,
> "Do not descry us for what is right;
> speak flatteries to us,
> conjure up illusions." (Is. 30, 10)

To impose silence on them is not enough. They must be got rid of:

> Out of our way! Out of our path!
> Let us hear no more of the Holy One of Israel. (Is. 30, 11)

Amaziah the priest of Bethel, after denouncing Amos to the king, tells him roughly to take his visions elsewhere:

Off with you, visionary,
flee to the land of Judah!
There earn your bread by prophesying,
but never again prophesy in Bethel,
for it is the king's sanctuary and a royal temple.
(Amos 7, 12-13)

Israel's feeling about the prophets is rather complex. For fear of having to believe them they call them madmen:

The prophet is a fool,
the man of the spirit is mad! (Hosea 9, 7)

They sneer knowingly at them:

To whom would he impart knowledge?
To whom would he convey the message?
To those just weaned from milk?
those taken from the breast? (Is. 28, 9)

At the same time there is fear of the word uttered in the name of Yahveh in case there may be some magic power attached to it. The latent hostility threatens at any moment to become open persecution:

Ephraim watches the prophet's tent;
a fowler's snare is on all his ways
hostility in the house of his God. (Hosea 9, 8)

Unable to get a hearing from Israel the prophet, like Christ after the failure of his preaching in Galilee, is obliged to confide his message to a handful of disciples:

The record is to be folded and the sealed instruction
kept among my disciples. (Is. 8, 16)

so that it may serve for the edification of future generations:

> Now come, write it on a tablet they can keep,
> inscribe it in a record;
> that it may be in future days an eternal witness. (Is. 30, 8)

The fact that the prophet is unwelcome as Yahveh's spokesman and that Israel rejects the messenger so as not to have to
accept the message has the result of making both the figure of
the prophet and his position in Israel exceptional. He very early
finds himself in the position of a man who is persecuted: Elijah's
flight, the imprisonment of Hanani and Micaiah the son of Imlah
are examples which continue with the experiences of Jeremiah
and John the Baptist and culminate in Christ. Connected with
this is his gradual isolation. Inevitably he is shunned by all:

> Alas! I am as when the fruit is gathered,
> as when the vines have been gleaned;
> there is no cluster to eat,
> no early fig that I crave!
> The faithful are gone from the earth,
> among men the upright are no more! (Micah 7, 1-2)

But if the prophet is isolated, it is so that he may remain un-
mistakably the *man of God* in the sight of the impenitent people.
He has been "separated" by Yahveh himself:

> For thus said Yahveh to me,
> when his hand took hold of me
> and he warned me not to walk in the way of this
> people. (Is. 11)

Amos had answered Amaziah the priest:

> I was no prophet, nor have I belonged to a company of

prophets. I was a shepherd and a dresser of sycamores. Yahveh took me from following the flock and said to me, "Go, prophesy to my people Israel." (Amos 7, 14-15)

Amos is referring to his former occupation before he became a prophet, but there is an obvious comparison with David who was also taken "from following the flock" of Israel. And while Israel refuses to submit to her God, the prophet submits obediently to the hand laid upon him. He seems to belong already to the world of the New Covenant and the world of grace that God creates with the hearts of those who accept his will. Isaiah is commanded to carry his word to Israel only after he has been cleansed by the burning coal of the seraphim.

Though more and more separated from his own people, the prophet however does not cease to feel his close kinship with them. His election does not let him forget that the precise aim of his mission is to work for their conversion, and he is only too grieved at their obduracy:

> For this reason I lament and wail,
> I go barefoot and naked;
> I utter lamentation like the jackals,
> and mourning like the ostriches,
> for there is no remedy for the blow she has
> been struck. (Micah 1, 8-9)

Even Isaiah loses his habitual serenity at the thought of it. While the crowds refuse to look for safety except in preparations for war, he goes and hides himself to groan in secret, like Christ weeping over Jerusalem:

> Turn away from me, let me weep bitterly;
> do not try to comfort me
> for the ruin of the daughter of my people. (Is. 22, 4)

Loyal to God and to the sinful world, the prophet is thus led to become an intermediary—the only person so qualified—between Yahveh and his people. Of his own accord he intervenes like Abraham to avert God's wrath:

> Forgive, O Lord God!
> How can Jacob stand?
> He is so small! (Amos 7, 2)

The role of intercessor places him at the center of the chosen people. He thus supplants the king who shares in Israel's sin and is thereby disqualified from the function that should have been his.

The authentic people of God, the "small remnant" who will receive God's word with humility, will be reformed around the prophet who, alone of all, has wholeheartedly chosen to remain under the hand of God, and thereby has deserved to be called by Yahveh himself his *Servant* (Is. 20, 3).

THE NEW TREND AMONG THE PROPHETS
ON THE EVE OF THE EXILE

5 When Manasseh became a vassal of the king of Assyria he did not hesitate to purchase peace at the price of servile collaboration. He felt no repugnance in introducing the star worship of Mesopotamia into the Temple itself, and installing the goddess Astarte, promoted to the rank of sister-spouse of Yahveh.

This was a hard blow dealt at the pure religion of Yahveh. It was all the more serious because during his reign apostasy seemed to be becoming general. New prophets were needed to rebuild the ruins of what their predecessors had so patiently constructed, another Hezekiah to repair the breach in the religious reform that had led to such high hopes. Though Josiah must be given all the credit for the reform of 622, he seems to have been able to impose it without much difficulty.

The reason for this is to be found in the fact that the work of the prophets in the eighth century had had a profound effect upon Israel—so profound that, after seeming rather precarious for a certain period, it turned out to be of lasting value. The people of God now knew that they had no guarantee of perpetual life. Hosea had made them realize that there was no salvation without love of God, and Isaiah that their communion with Yahveh could be reestablished only by acceptance of purification. Breaking with the cyclic beliefs common to the East, they had

now accepted a "linear" conception of events, and had become
aware that the destiny of Israel was the living of a unique and
ever-progressing adventure under the guidance of Yahveh's hand.

The undeniable influence of the prophets made itself felt
in the whole life of the nation. The liturgy gave so great importance to the feast of the Pasch that the ancient agrarian rites
were relegated to a second place, and it is probable that the
proclamation of the kingship of Yahveh was accompanied by a
new renewal of the Covenant. The legal system reflected the
messages of Hosea and Isaiah, who had adapted Deuteronomy
and the Code of Holiness (*Lev.* 17-26) to everyday needs. This influence is to be found even in the compilation of sacred history
on which the popular imagination was fed. In short, it may be
said that the furrow dug by the prophets was far from being
a simple scratching of the soil; there was no need of further
plowing.

Yet when Jeremiah's voice was heard three quarters of a
century after those of the great prophets had become silent, it
seems that he is only reechoing the teaching of his predecessors.
At least this is the first impression the modern reader gets from
his early utterances. The familiar themes of the eighth century
are all there: sacred prostitutes in the high places, Israel's
adultery, the vineyard laid waste, the cleansing fire. It might be
said that Jeremiah was trying to rouse them from forgetfulness.
This is doubtless partly true, for Manasseh and Amon for fifty
years had done their best to revive the errors denounced by
Hosea and the vices scourged by Isaiah:

> Roam the streets of Jerusalem,
> look about and observe,
> search through her public places,
> to find even one who lives uprightly,
> and seeks to be faithful. (Jer. 5, 1)

But it is only a passing attitude. When examined more closely,

these old themes are seen to have no more than a literary significance. They have lost their freshness and vigor; the imagery
is rather worn. In any case, the interest of his message does not
lie in this. Far from remaining static, the message of the prophets
from Jeremiah onwards advances resolutely in a new direction.
Its context becomes, on the one hand, more interior and on the
other more universal.

*   *   *

Amos, Hosea and Isaiah were traditional prophets in the sense
that they took their cue from circumstances and pointed out to
the nation what their behavior ought to be in the face of particular events. In the framework of the Old Covenant they interpreted the wishes of Yahveh in the cases that occurred.

The prophets who came after them, however, were to enlarge
the range of their message. They were less concerned with immediate events than with Israel's attitude to the Word delivered
to them in the name of Yahveh. Besides realizing that the chosen
people now stood condemned, and that therefore it was useless
to urge them to placate divine justice with a repentance that had
never been quite sincere or lasting, they were forcibly struck by
the fact that, as far as actual events showed, Israel had always
remained deaf to reproaches and exhortations. She had shown
a deep-rooted and persistent lack of submissiveness which was
to lead fatally to the breaking of the Covenant, and as a consequence to the final ruin of the chosen people. How could it be
possible for the design of Yahveh to be accomplished in such
circumstances? It is on this problem that Jeremiah concentrates
his attention, and after him Ezekiel and the second Isaiah. They
are thus drawn to glimpse the only solution capable of safe-
guarding the divine plan: the establishment of a *New Covenant*
made on *new bases*.

There is also a modification in their conception of Israel's
sin. The eighth century prophets certainly had no hesitation

in defining it. For Amos it is a transgression of the terms of the Covenant. For Hosea it is infidelity to divine love. Isaiah sees it as man's impurity. Rightly so, they had emphasized the nature of it that best fitted in with their teaching. By doing so, however, they had given rather too narrow a sense to the violation of moral and religious laws. From Jeremiah onwards, sin assumes a wider and deeper significance. The prophets of the new generation are concerned with showing the essential gravity of sin rather than with presenting it under one particular aspect.

With Jeremiah, for example, sin is nothing else but a *perversion of the moral sense.* He judges it as we ourselves would judge it. Worship in the high places is not a profanation of love nor a violation of the Covenant, but plain and simple idolatry. Sacred prostitution and the sacrifice of the first-born are not signs of lack of faith but of moral corruption and wickedness.

Seen from this angle, sin could not be corrected by a simple return to ways that had been abandoned. It would no longer be enough to submit to the obligations of the Covenant, or to respond to Yahveh's love, or even to let oneself be cleansed by trial and suffering, for the root, cause of sin, would not thereby be cured. The source itself would have to be cleansed. In other words, it was not man's behavior that needed reforming, but man himself that had to be changed. Hence instead of "Obey!" or "Return love for love!" or "Believe!" Jeremiah was to say, "Be converted!":

> For twenty three years the word of the Lord has come to me and I spoke to you untiringly ... with this message: Turn back, each of you from your evil way and from your evil deeds. (Jer. 25, 3-5)

In the circumstances, it is easy to understand why this call to conversion should be addressed less to the collectivity than to the individuals composing it. It was no longer a case of persuading the nation to conform its religious, social or political policy to the will of Yahveh, as interpreted or revealed by the prophets, but to awaken the consciences and change the hearts of man. The interpretation that the new prophets were giving to the external situation was furthermore to contribute to under-lining in their message this tendency to individualize the religion of Israel.

The eighth century prophets had emphasized the presence of God's hand in the events by which he wished to lead his people back to him. They explained the Assyrian invasion, the Syro-Ephraimite war and Sennacherib's raid on Jerusalem as lessons from God. Jeremiah and his successors, however, proclaim that this time Israel is being swept away by an irresistible force from which nothing can save her, and that Yahveh's decision admits neither of appeal nor delay. Disaster will take its inevitable course and nothing can stop it. There will be another invasion and a siege with all its horrors, as well as the storming and sacking of the city with the slaughter of its inhabitants. The temple will be profaned, pillaged and burnt to the ground and the survivors led away as prisoners with the king in chains at their head. Yahveh will abandon his holy city, his temple and his kingly house. The outlook for the future is hopeless. Israel as a political entity and military power will be wiped off the map.

Their only course is to submit and accept the certainty of their fate. Those who can will return to Yahveh by the path of humiliation and dispersion. Israel will no longer be a nation, but each one of them will himself become Israel. *Each one will have to respond individually to the call of Yahveh.*

✿   ✿   ✿

However, though Jeremiah and the other prophets of the seventh and sixth centuries treat external events as of secondary importance and see in them only a further reason for laying stress on the need for interior conversion, nonetheless their eyes are fixed on the world around them. Before their time the gentile nations were simply regarded as a scourge wielded by the avenging arm of Yahveh. Like their predecessors, they too announce that the proud empires will come to ruin in their turn— if they were to survive the ruin of Israel, in the eyes of the world Yahveh would seem to be a defeated god, which would be unthinkable.

But—and this is a second novelty, of no less importance than the first—these nations, like Israel, will be replanted when the time comes, for they too will benefit in some way from the promises of the living God. Thus, *the prophet's mission now begins to extend to the whole world*:

> I set you over nations and over kingdoms,
> to root up and to tear down,
> to destroy and to demolish,
> to build and to plant. (Jer. 1, 10)

While the new Jerusalem—a Jerusalem transfigured by the *Shûb Shebût*, the return of the exiles—remains the focal point of the prophet's vision, at the same time the holy city becomes the spiritual center of the world, to which the nations will flock in admiration:

> At that time they will call Jerusalem "the Throne of Yahveh"; there all nations will be gathered together in the name of Yahveh, and they will walk no longer in their hard-hearted wickedness. (Jer. 3, 17)

Zephaniah was to speak more clearly still:

> For then I will change and purify the lips of the peoples, that they all may call upon the name of Yahveh, to serve him with one accord. (Zeph. 3, 9)

By the very fact that it is addressed to individuals rather than to the nation as a whole, the preaching of the prophets tends to become modified both in method and form. To obtain a hearing from the community they had until now found it natural to take advantage of the liturgical solemnities—the festival of Yahveh, for example—when they wished to speak. Their sayings were usually brief and in verse-form, as the crowd would be more impressed by rythmic utterance with concise and forcible phrases able to attract their attention, strike the imagination and remain in the memory. At the beginning of his ministry Jeremiah had followed the custom of his predecessors and had risen in the midst of popular festal gatherings to disturb them with his invectives. It can be noticed, however, that his style becomes less vigorous and the mode of expression more wordy. But the day came when he could no longer deliver his message in public. Isaiah before him had had to limit his ministry to forming a handful of disciples and even sometimes to dictating his prophecies. Jeremiah had no other resource but to write down his. Ezekiel was obliged to do the same from the need to circulate his message among the dispersed exiles. The poems of the second Isaiah definitely lack all trace of oral composition. The Word of God tends gradually to become a *Book*.

Thus a progressive change can be seen in the prophetic function from what it was in origin, as regards both object and exterior form. With Jeremiah it reaches a turning point that was bound to lead to its disappearance. Once the New Covenant had made it clear that each person was to be responsible for his own fidelity and that trust in God was to be a personal matter, there would be more need of directors of conscience for the individual than of guides for the community. The prophecy as an institution would disappear and its place be taken by the *Qahal* (assembly) of Wise Men.

JEREMIAH

6 Jeremiah was born in the last years of the reign of Manasseh (687-641). He belonged to a family of priests living at Anathoth, a village to the north of Jerusalem. His prophetic vocation dates from the year 626, shortly before the great religious reform of 622 carried out under King Josiah.

The decline of Assyria after the death of Assurbanipal (625) made a complete change of policy possible both in diplomacy and religion. The moment seemed ripe for throwing off the century-long yoke of subjection to Nineveh. But a new power, the Babylon of Nabopolassar (626-605), was in the ascendant. Allying themselves with the Medes, the Chaldeans hastened on the fall of the great kingdom which had lorded it over the East for centuries. Assyria fell in 614, and in 612 it was the turn of Nineveh. Foreseeing the danger from Babylon, Pharaoh Necho II decided to come to the aid of the remaining Assyrians. Josiah tried to bar his way, but with disastrous results, being defeated and slain at Megiddo in 609. Such was the tragic end of the great reforming king, one of the most upright men to reign in Jerusalem after David.

Jehoiakim (609-598) was set on the throne of his father by the Pharaoh himself. The latter, however, was defeated in his turn by Nebuchadnezzar at Carchemish (605), but the victor was too occupied elsewhere to advance into Palestine at once. He waited until 598 before laying siege to Jerusalem. King Jehoiakim, who had inauguarated the pro-Egyptian policy, had just died and his young son, Jehoiachin, paid the penalty for his father's error. The city was captured and the king deported to Babylon with the élite of the population.

Josiah's last remaining son was placed on the throne by Nebuchadnezzar and took the name of Zedekiah. Under the influence of the pro-Egyptian party he entered into a new coalition against Babylon. Retribution came swiftly. Jerusalem was besieged in January 588 but managed to hold out till July of the following year. Jeremiah had always supported a policy of non-resistance to Babylon and was not carried away captive with the bulk of the population. After the assassination of Gedaliah, the governor of Jerusalem, a group of Jews who feared fresh reprisals forced him to accompany them into Egypt. There the great prophet who had announced the end of the Old Covenant met an obscure death.

A.—ISRAEL REJECTS THE HAND OF GOD

After a millennium and a half of life, the mighty Assyrian empire which had extended its dominion from the Persian Gulf to the borders of Ethiopia, destroying the kingdom of Samaria and making Judah its vassal, was now tottering to its fall and would never rise again. Sennacherib and Assurbanipal still continued to act as if they were great kings. They had both ruthlessly suppressed Babylon's attempts at independence, but their successors lacked their spirit and determination. By 626 they were powerless to prevent hordes of Scythians from ravaging the eastern part of the empire, and Babylon, where in the same year Nabopolassar founded the Chaldean dynasty, suddenly awoke to life. Her armies defeated the Assyrians at Arapha in 615, and the following year the Medes gained possession of Assur. Joining their forces, Chaldeans and Medes inflicted a series of severe defeats on the Assyrian king, Sir-Shar-Iskun, before laying siege to Nineveh in 612. The city was taken, sacked and razed to the ground, and the inhabitants slaughtered. Assur-Uballit made a vain attempt to rally the Assyrian forces; they were routed at Carchemish in 609, and Assyria ceased to exist.

There was agreat feeling of relief among the small vassal states, at least in the period between the destruction of Nineveh and the battle of Carchemish. Nahum expresses the delirious joy that swept through Jerusalem at the time, when independence seemed to have at last been regained:

See, upon the mountain there advances the bearer of good news, announcing peace! Celebrate your feasts, O Judah!
(Nahum 2, 1)

But it did not take long for the rejoicing to subside. After a brief period of Egyptian domination Palestine fell in 605 into the hands of the new masters who were to impose their law for more than sixty years. With Nebuchadnezzar, Nineveh's place was taken by Babylon.

An Amos or an Isaiah would not have failed to find matter to excite their imagination and reinforce their message in events of such momentous nature. Only a few years before Jeremiah, Zephaniah—following the style of the prophets before him— sees Yahveh descending in the midst of the storm and whirlwind and manifesting himself much as he did on Sinai:

Near is the great day of Yahveh,
near, and very swiftly coming.
Hark, the day of Yahveh!
Bitter, then, the warrior's cry.
A day of wrath is that day,
a day of anguish and distress,
a day of destruction and desolation,

a day of darkness and gloom,
a day of thick black clouds. (Zeph. 1, 14-15)

Probably his predecessors would have believed, as Zephaniah did, in yet another possibility of forgiveness:

Seek justice, seek humility:
perhaps you may be sheltered
on the day of Yahveh's anger. (Zeph. 2, 3)

But Jeremiah's eyes are fixed, not on these tragic events, but on a drama of quite another kind:

— What do you see, Jeremiah?
— I see a branch of the watching-tree (= almond tree).
— Well have you seen, for I am watching to fulfill my word.
(Jer. 1, 11-12)

For the dire promise will be fulfilled without fail. Israel had come gradually to fear no longer Yahveh's repeated threats, for the least sign of repentance was enough for him to pardon them. Yahveh's patience, though long-lasting, will not be eternal. He is tired of the trickeries of his beloved (11, 15) and still more of her infidelities. The stork, the swallow and thrush return faithfully when their season comes round (8, 7); the snow has never been known to desert the tops of Lebanon (18, 14). It is only Israel that does not remember God, without whom she cannot live:

My people have forgotten me
days without number. (2, 32)

She has rejected the saving hand of God and turned aside from him:

You have disowned me (says the Lord),
turned your back upon me. (15, 6; cf. 2, 19, 27)

It is much more than simple forgetfulness or thoughtlessness.
Israel has risen up against her God, and not for the first time:

Long ago you broke your yoke,
you tore off your bonds.
"I will not serve," you said. (2, 20; cf. 5, 5)

In his merciful patience Yahveh has always respected the
Covenant in spite of all the infidelities of his people:

Why do my people say:
"We have moved on,
we will come to you no more"? (2, 31)

What fault did your fathers find in me
that they withdrew from me? (2, 5)

But since Israel persists in betraying her God, he will withdraw from his people:

I will show you mercy no longer. (16, 13)

Yahveh will rid himself of a useless burden (23, 33). In fact
he has already done so:

I have forsaken my house,
cast off my heritage. (12, 7)

He has given up his vineyard and will let it be ravaged with
indifference:

Tear away her tendrils,
they do not belong to Yahveh. (5, 10)

With God's departure Israel will remain with her sin and
this will be her punishment:

Your own wickedness chastises you,
your own infidelities punish you. (2, 19)

The great hopes founded on the kingship of Yahveh in Zion
are at an end. Though priests and people at the coronation of
Jehoiakim are loud in celebration of the inviolability of Jerusalem, though to reassure themselves they cry:

This is the temple of Yahveh! the temple of Yahveh! the
temple of Yahveh! (7, 4)

They are only deceiving themselves with lying words, for there
is no foundation for their belief:

I will treat this house like Shiloh,
and make this the city which all the nations of the earth shall
refer to when cursing another. (26, 6)

The royal line of David will die out with Jehoiakim whose
corpse shall soon be cast out "exposed to the heat of day, the
cold of night" (36, 30); and the state with all its traditional
structure will collapse at the same time as the monarchy:

I will fill with drunkenness all the inhabitants of this land,
the kings who succeed to David's throne, the priests and
prophets, and all the citizens of Jerusalem. I will dash them
against each other, fathers and sons together (Yahveh says);
I will show no compassion, I will not spare or pity, but will
destroy them. (13, 13-14)

Israel cannot hope to obtain anything by hypocritical worship. God is not mocked. When they sing in the Temple:

We are called by your name. (14, 9)

what else is it but derision? Does not the sacred name sound like a false oath on their lips?

Though they say, "As the Lord lives," they swear falsely.
(5, 2)

However much the prophets may intercede, Yahveh will remain deaf:

Do not intercede for this people. (14, 11)

Even if Moses and Samuel stood before me, my heart would not turn toward this people. Cast them out of my sight and let them go forth. (15, 1)

If a man puts away his wife and she marries another, can she be taken back by her first husband? (3, 1). Jerusalem will be ruthlessly cast away on the rubbish heap like the vessel the potter destroys because it has turned out badly (18, 4-6) and like the broken flask that cannot be repaired (19, 10-11).

It will not be long, however, before the people will open their eyes. Then they will realize that the severance is final and complete and will say in astonishment:

Is Yahveh no longer in Zion?
Is her king no longer in her midst? (8, 19)

The answer will come:

The covenant I made with their fathers, the house of Israel and the house of Judah have broken. (11, 10)

The clear-sighted will recognize with Jeremiah that the threats of death in the message of the prophets of old were the tangible signs of this severance. What strikes Jeremiah most is the terrible pity of it. No other prophet shows such intense feeling and compassion for the fate Israel has brought upon herself by her refusal to accept God's love. Memories of the times never to return crowd into his mind, reminding him of the joyful espousals of the Lord with his people:

I remember the devotion of your youth,
how you loved me as a bride,
following me in the desert,
in a land unsown. (2, 2)

In those days Israel was sacred to God and no one would have dared to lay a hand on her with impunity:

Sacred to Yahveh was Israel,
the first fruits of his harvest.
Should anyone presume to partake of them,
evil would befall him. (2, 3)

Still more, while being the glory of his people, Yahveh himself received glory from Israel:

As close as the loincloth clings to a man's loins, so had I made the whole house of Israel and the whole house of Judah cling to me, to be my people, my renown, my praise, my glory. (13, 11)

Had not Israel, who now goes saying to idols of wood and stone "You are my father" (2, 27), had the extraordinary privilege of being regarded by Yahveh as his son?

You would call me "My Father," I thought,
and never cease following me. (3, 19)

All this extraordinary intimacy is now lost, and of how much has Israel thus been deprived! A new Adam, he has shut himself out of the garden in which God showered every blessing upon him. Yahveh had been an inexhaustible fountain for them:

They have forsaken me, the source of living waters. (2, 13)

The inhabitants of Palestine knew only too well the value of water springs not to guard them jealously, but this one has been despised by Israel in order to dig themselves

cisterns, broken cisterns, that hold no water. (2, 13)

So life exists no longer. Dead and gone are the happy days of peaceful labor and innocent joys, the quiet evenings of family activity:

Before your very eyes and during your lifetime
I will silence from this place
the cry of joy and the cry of gladness,
the voice of the bridegroom and the voice of the bride,
the sound of the millstone and the light of the lamp.
(16, 9; 25, 10)

Dead are the liturgical ceremonies the splendor of which filled with wonder the childhood of the prophet, a priest and the son of a priest. Dead, the pilgrimages, the thanksgivings, the dancing to the tambourine. And this death, already approaching, will lay its icy hand on those for whom life has hardly begun:

Death has come up through our windows,
has entered our palaces;
it cuts down the children in the street,
young people in the squares.
The corpses of the slain lie like dung on a field,

like sheaves behind the harvester,
with no one to gather them. (9, 20-21)

Then, when the bitter wind blows from the east, dispersing
like grains of sand those who have survived the massacre, and
they will have to leave their homes, fields and vineyards to the
invader (6, 12), they will be like a dying man who sees all that
he has accumulated, possessed and loved on earth slipping away
from his exhausted hands. And their bondage in a foreign land
where everything will be hostile to them and where they will
drag out a miserable existence will be like the mournful state
of the dead in Sheol (16, 13; 5, 19).

Nature itself will become rebellious to the rebellious people.
The rain will fall no more, the springing corn will wither from
drought and thorns grow in its place, while the plowman will
cover his head in shame at the sight of the harvest he goes to
reap (3, 3; 12, 13). Nor could it be otherwise, for the whole land
is defiled—defiled by the abominations of Israel (2, 7), defiled
by her "harlotry and wickedness" (3, 2), defiled by the corpses of
the slain that lie scattered in the fields (9, 21). The land vomits
with horror those it once nourished, and the towns, widowed
of their inhabitants (2, 15), have become a heap of ruins,
a dwelling place of jackals (9, 11). Even if some places are
spared, the people will not dare to step outside them for fear
of being torn to pieces by wild beasts—wolves, leopards and
lions—that lie in wait close at hand. The birds of the air and the
beasts of the field have all fled and gone (9, 9).

There will be nothing to console Israel for the loss of her
God, for even the good earth will withdraw its friendship. They
will go wandering through a stricken land under a sky ever dark
(4, 28). Everywhere their feet will stumble on "mountains of
darkness" (13, 16), and all will return to original chaos:

I looked at the earth, and it was waste and void;
at the heavens, and their light had gone out!

I looked at the mountains and they were trembling,
and all the hills were crumbling!
I looked and behold, there was no man;
even the birds of the air had flown away!
I looked and behold, the garden land was a desert,
with all its cities destroyed. (4, 23-26)

While sustaining Israel, the hand of Yahveh also sustained the
world in which they lived. Having lost God, they lost everything
—"Unless the Lord build the house, they labor in vain that build
it" (Ps. 127, 1).

B.—CIRCUMCISION OF THE HEART

At the beginning of his mission Isaiah had cried:

I live among a people of unclean lips. (Is. 6, 5)

When Jeremiah realizes the incurable perversion of Israel, he
apparently says the same thing:

You walk, every one of you, in the hardness of your evil
heart. (Jer. 16, 12)

But Jeremiah seeks the source of this uncleanness which
Isaiah denounces and finds it in human nature itself. There is
therefore on this point in the thought of the prophets a huge
step forward which was to have far-reaching consequences.

         ✺   ✺   ✺

Amos, Hosea and Isaiah had proclaimed that Yahveh guided
the destinies of his people with a hand that was both heavy and
merciful. They had also stated on what terms Yahveh would save
them from the fatal perils to which they exposed themselves so
lightheartedly. He demanded of them that they should uncon-

ditionally forsake their. abominations and surrender themselves
exclusively to the divine will.

In moments of crisis Israel had indeed come to realize that
it was only on their God they could rely. They had allowed themselves to be guided by him, but only half-heartedly, while
refusing to abandon the path they had so short-sightedly chosen:

No one repents of his wickedness,
saying, "What have I done!"
Everyone keeps on running his course. (8, 6)

Threatened by imminent danger they were ready enough to
acknowledge Yahveh as their king, but their submission was only
a pretense. God could hardly rely on such inconstant and super-
ficial collaboration to carry out his design.

You are upon their lips but far from their thoughts. (12, 2)

Of what use is it to invoke the thrice-holy name if the mind
and heart belie what the lips pronounce? Israel may still continue to swear by the living God, but they do not do so "in truth,
in judgment, and in justice" (4, 2).

Words and gestures only have value from the intention and
feelings of the person who uses them; when it comes to obeying,
Israel is deaf to the voice of her God:

Their ears are uncircumcised,
they cannot give heed. (6, 10)

After offering sacrifice in the Temple they think they have
done their duty to Yahveh, but if conduct should be an expression
of inward piety, their failings cannot but be evident:

They set their faces harder than stone. (5, 3)

They have shamelessly accustomed themselves to this kind of double game. At the very moment that they piously address Yahveh as "My Father!" they are sinking further into crime:

This is what you say, yet you do all the evil you can. (3, 5)

What can be done to bring Israel back to sincere obedience? Amos had threatened them with the worst calamities. Hosea saw no other solution but a return to the desert. Isaiah relied on purification by fire. But these were only palliatives, and very imperfect ones at that. If Israel persists in her absolute refusal to obey, even though attentive to minute details of worship, neither the inevitable chastisements, nor the harsh lessons of the desert, nor cleansing through trials will make her such as Yahveh wishes her, such as she must become in order to realize God's design:

Can vows and sacred meat turn away your misfortune from you? (11, 15)

Jeremiah, chosen by God as "the tester of his people" takes note of this impossible situation:

The bellows roar,
the lead is consumed by the fire;
in vain has the smelter refined,
the dross is not drawn off. (6, 29)

This discouraging observation is confirmed by Yahveh himself:

Though you scrub it with soap,
and use much bleach,
the stain of your guilt is still before me. (2, 22)

After the failure of his preaching during the reign of Jehoiakim, Jeremiah goes so far as to ask himself the despairing question:

Can the Ethiopian change his skin?
the leopard his spots?
As easily would you be able to do good,
accustomed to evil as you are. (13, 23)

There is here a vicious circle from which there is no way of escape. It is useless for God to keep on extending the date of payment, for the debtor is insolvent. The only conclusion is that Israel is unsuited for what God expects of her.

In these circumstances it is difficult to see how the religion of Moses and David, the same religion as that of Hosea and Isaiah, could continue to survive. It might seem doomed to disappear, like the other religions of antiquity, now that the Covenant had proved a failure through Israel's fault. As a national religion, it should have been swept away at the same time as the kingdom of Judah in the storm then gathering which was to absorb the small states into the great empires.

* * *

But it is now that Jeremiah shows the people of Israel how they may find God's hand again. Renan's judgment on him still bears quotation: *"Sans cet homme extraordinaire, l'histoire religieuse de l'humanité eût suivi un autre cours."* This "extraordinary man" was raised up by Yahveh at the right moment, after his predecessors had traced the path he would take.

As Jeremiah sees it, Yahveh is forsaking Israel only because he does not find sufficient submission. To be effective his dominion must be complete, and man must dedicate himself to God without reserve. The part of him that Yahveh wishes to reach is his *heart*. To belong to God, his heart must not only be subdued by adversity but must be converted. This is what Israel refuses to do.

They have refused to return to you. (5, 3)

What is the meaning of this "be converted"? It does not mean outward submission to the demands of a jealous God, such as he appears in the Old Testament and especially in Hosea and Isaiah—jealous in such a way as no ancient religion would have been capable of imagining. Nor does it mean full adhesion to a doctrine and the punctual exercise of good works deriving from it, the most that was required by religious systems outside of the Judaeo-Christian tradition. To speak of conversion in the case of the latter is to set quite a different interpretation on the meaning of the word. Islam, for example, requires the believer to pay exclusive worship to Allah, but this exclusiveness implies nothing more than that a man should belong in a certain measure to his God, and imposes neither a radical change in the deeper dispositions of the soul, nor the total surrender of the heart. Yet it is here that conversion begins. It does not attack evil in its effects, but at its root.

This is the kind of conversion of which Jeremiah speaks:

Cleanse your heart of evil, O Jerusalem,
that you may be saved. (4, 14)

He expresses it in a bold metaphor that St. Paul was later to re-echo:

For Yahveh's sake, be circumcised,
remove the foreskins of your hearts. (4, 4)

Leaving imagery aside, conversion is a death and a rebirth:

the death of the perverse heart, the rebirth of a faithful one. Here we come back again to the connection between the ideas of death and resurrection that had struck humanity from earliest times, suggested by the spectacle of nature. It inspires all the primitive cyclic cults, to which up to the time of Isaiah Israel was no exception. But neither this death nor this rebirth are final. Nothing in nature disappears except to begin again. Nothing is reborn except to die again.

It is one of Isaiah's chief merits to have shown that human history is not governed by the same laws as nature, and to have been able to free the religious thought of Israel from a closed circle by showing a vision of a straight line starting from Sinai and leading to Mount Zion. He displayed before the eyes of the journeying people, in spite of the obstacles that lay in their path, the approach to the kingdom of eternal peace and universal harmony where Yahveh the King would have his reign. Though the purification that marks the final stage implies the necessity of a death, it is only a partial one in the sense that it spares "the remnant," and where it strikes, it does not seem to have to be followed by any rebirth. When the dross is destroyed, only the pure gold remains at the bottom of the crucible.

Going further than Isaiah, Jeremiah more strongly emphasizes and more clearly delineates the sequence by which any given death must necessarily be followed by a resurrection, and affirms the general character of this law as applying both to the individual and the nation. He keeps the idea of "the remnant," but in the sense of a leaven that will raise the new bread rather than of the precious metal remaining after the work of the smelter. It is for this reason that he calls impatiently for the death of the old heart and the old people, to hasten the moment when the dawn of a moral resurrection will break.

We have seen how intensely he invoked this death. At the time of Sennacherib's invasion Isaiah loudly proclaimed his faith in the inviolability of Zion, while Jeremiah never ceases to proclaim the inevitable destruction of all that once was. Though timid by nature, none of the very real dangers that threatened him could prevent him from delivering his message.

Already by 605 entrance to the Temple was denied him. He was beaten and pilloried, and had to go into hiding to escape being murdered. During the siege of Jerusalem he was persecuted under a charge of defeatism. He remained undaunted, proclaiming that all resistance to Nebuchadnezzar only served to delay the hour of revival. While a prisoner and with everything to fear, he still gave the same answer five times to Zedekiah when he came to consult him: submission to Babylon, for there can be no restoration without first accepting defeat. New wine cannot be put into old jars.

But rebirth is not less certain than death. This is the significance of the two baskets of figs before which the prophet stands in meditation after the first capture of Jerusalem by Nebuchadnezzar. The first basket contains only bad figs: these are the Jews who have remained in Jerusalem and who imagine they will benefit by the promises of the Covenant, while in reality they belong to a world which has vanished. In the second basket the figs are ripe and good: these are the exiles, those who no longer form part of the doomed kingdom; they will receive a new heart and so have a right to look hopefully to the future:

Like these good figs, even so will I regard with favor Judah's exiles whom I sent away from this place into the land of the Chaldeans. I will look after them for their good, and bring them back to this land, to build them up, not to tear them down, to plant them, not to pluck them out. I will give them a heart with which to understand that I am Yahveh. They shall be my people and I shall be their God, for they shall return to me with their whole heart. (24, 5-7)

The more thorough the destruction, the more complete will be the restoration:

I will take delight in doing good to them; I will replant them firmly in this land, with all my heart and soul. . . . Just as I brought upon this people all this great evil, so I will bring upon them all the good I promise them. (32, 41-42)

The buying of land in Anathoth—his native region—which the prophet undertakes by order of Yahveh has no other sense:

Fields shall again be bought in this land, which you call a desert, without man or beast, handed over to the Chaldeans . . . for I will cause their captivity to return. (32, 43-44)

Yahveh will then gather together the scattered sheep into a new flock. He will lead them into their folds and will appoint shepherds over them:

They need no longer fear and tremble,
and none shall be missing. (23, 4)

The God who is able to destroy everything can also make everything rearise from nothingness:

Behold, I am Yahveh, the God of all flesh.
Is anything impossible to me? (32, 27)

❋   ❋   ❋

The conversion announced by Jeremiah, as can be seen, takes no account of the old religious values to which Israel attached so much importance. The Temple, the holy city, the Davidic monarchy may disappear, for these traditional bases of the Hebrew state are not indispensable for God's design. The prophet had been able to preserve intimacy with God outside of the Temple from which he had been excluded. Yahveh is not confined to one place; He can be found everywhere if one looks deep into one's heart. There will be no more need to carry away, as Naaman the leper did in the time of Elisha, some of the soil of Palestine in order to be able to invoke Yahveh. And so Jeremiah counsels the exiles to settle in Babylon as though they would never return, and to seek Yahveh there:

> Promote the walfare of the city to which I have exiled you; pray for it to Yahveh.... When you call me, when you go to pray to me, I will listen to you. When you look for me you will find me. Yes, when you seek me with all your heart, you will find me with you. (29, 7-14)

This new people will be formed only by men with new hearts. Their religion will be *personal*, by joining to God not the nation as a single whole, but the individuals comprising the nation. It will also be *interior*, because words and actions will respond to the sincerity and fidelity of the heart.

It should be noted that this evolution, which was to detach the human person from the collective mass, had already had a beginning in Israel before Jeremiah, at least in a juridical sense. In the eighth century King Amaziah in punishing the murderers of his father had upheld the principle of individual retribution by condemning them to death but not their children (2 Kings 14, 5-6). But this innovation had only a legal aspect and had yet to become a moral and religious principle. The credit is due to Jeremiah of having posed the question. By preaching a religion that demanded submission of the heart, he was bound to conclude that henceforth each individual would be responsible for his personal fidelity:

> In those days they shall no longer say,
> "The fathers ate unripe grapes,

and the children's teeth are set on edge,"
but through his own fault only shall anyone die:
the teeth of him who eats the unripe grapes shall set on edge.

(31, 29-30)

Conversion, in short, presupposes a personal decision, and if they wish to remain the holy people, Israel must become a people of holy persons.

Man by himself is incapable of giving God the heart which God wishes to be his. The heart of flesh that he has inside him is too heavy and too hard to be sensible to divine influence. It is necessary for God to create this new heart in him:

with which to understand that I am Yahveh. (24, 7)

Yahveh will engrave his law in it more deeply than on the stone of the tables of Moses:

I will place my law within them, and write it upon their hearts; I will be their God and they shall be my people. No longer will they have need to teach their friends and kinsmen how to know Yahveh. All, from least to greatest, shall know me. (31, 33-34)

If Yahveh will completely change man's heart, the reason is that it is completely perverse. When Jeremiah discerns the depth of sin and from it concludes the need for divine intervention, manifesting itself in a spiritual life nourished by God alone, he discovers a new relationship, that between *sin* and *grace*. In this he foreshadows St. Paul, as in the well-known passage where the apostle compares the universality of the salvation brought by Christ to the universality of original sin. Both in the prophet and in the apostle the same thought is to be found: grace penetrates to the very bottom of the abyss dug by sin and pursues it to the very end; one seems to call to the other. But while the prophet considers only the individual and the conversion of the heart, the apostle has all men in mind and affirms the universality of the redemption—the substitution in each person of the old man for the new.

Isaiah sees Sinai as the beginning of God's special action, and he interprets the final victory of Yahveh the King on the holy mountain as the accomplishment of the Old Covenant. Jeremiah looks further afield. Behind him he sees creation as the origin of God's intervention, and ahead of him a kind of second creation, which will also have its covenant, an eternal one, engraved in the hearts of a transfigured Israel.

Jeremiah is, in fact, the first of the prophets to allude to the *creation*. Though the reference in not strongly marked, it cannot be ignored:

Thus says Yahveh,
he who gives the sun to light the day,
moon and stars to light the night,
who stirs up the sea till its waves roar,
whose name is Lord of hosts:
If ever these ordinances give way in spite of me,
then shall the race of Israel cease as a nation
before me forever. (31, 35-36)

The *New Covenant* that Yahveh proposes demands a personal consent of which only a renewed heart is capable. Israel will be then not only his people but the community of his faithful ones. The holy nation will extend its confines far beyond the narrow boundaries of its geographical position. It will include all its children scattered through a large empire before spreading through the world.

Jeremiah affirms the necessity of the death of the old incorrigible people as a necessary condition for their resurrection, and he enunciates the principle of a new worship that shall no longer be formalistic and collective, but interior and individual. He thus makes it eminently possible for this worship to be inserted into the new world that was being born with the Greek city, a world in which the *human person* was to assert itself by shaking free of its former sociological servitude and setting the seal of liberty on thought and art no less than on philosophical and religious ideas. Thus, at the very moment it was being threatened with extinction the religion of Israel found a new source of life and vigor which was to carry it throughout the world once it had been impregnated with Christianity.

C.—THE PERSONAL EXPERIENCE OF JEREMIAH AS THE TESTING GROUND OF THE NEW COVENANT

The old Israel, now on the point of extinction, had received the Covenant of Sinai as a collective law, meant to regulate the social, moral and religious behavior of the community. The New Covenant announced by Jeremiah was to be a spiritual charter, binding on the heart of each particular person, and the new people would be a number of individual states of fidelity woven together. Such is the new form taken by God's design.

But before this New Covenant could come into operation, Yahveh had to create a model of the man that was to come, one who would serve as a standard for the individuals of the future community. This community when formed would become a model community from which, as on a ground ready to receive the seed of his word, the new Lawgiver would make the new people.

This model man should be absolutely faithful to the terms of the Old Covenant by unhesitating obedience to God's will in following the path along which God wished to lead him. In addition he would have to suffer the ordeal of isolation, and thereby be freed from a world that was ceasing to exist, and be taught the secret of true intimacy with God.

The man who was to have the great privilege of living this experience and the credit of not allowing it to fail was Jeremiah.

The religious life of Israel, centered as it was on the monarchy, could be summed up to a certain extent in the personality of its *king*. Independently of his political power, his anointing gave him a twofold character: he was the representative and the Son of Yahveh on earth, and the spokesman for his people with Yahveh. It was he who on occasions of national rejoicing gave him thanks in the name of all. It was likewise him who recited public lamentation in times of trouble or disaster such as famine, plague and war. All the trials of his people became his personally. When he addressed Yahveh he was the voice of Israel, responsible for expressing the nation's gratitude, praying for divine protection, interceding for them in their misfortune and transgressions. As the authorized leader of the people he was bound to rule them with faith and justice. According as he did "that which is just or that which is evil in the sight of Yahveh" he was rewarded or punished both in his own person or in his people, as both were a single entity. In this respect the Jewish king enjoyed the privileges and bore the responsibilities that the ancient world attributed to monarchy by reason of its religious character.

From the eighth century, however, there had been a tendency for this primacy to desert the kings of Israel in favor of the prophets, messengers of the divine word. With the ministry of Jeremiah this process of gradual substitution reaches its final phase.

We find, for example, the prophet taking upon himself the suffering of Israel:

I am broken by the ruin of the daughter of my people.
I am disconsolate. Horror has seized me. (8, 21)

When he groans and weeps he does so in the name of the whole people as though he, and he alone, is their representative.

> Let my eyes stream with tears,
> day and night without rest,
> over the great destruction which overwhelms the virgin daughter of my people,
> over her incurable wound. (14, 17)

His expression of his people's woe is, however, the result of his own intense personal experience:

> My breast! my breast! how I suffer!
> The walls of my heart!
> My heart beats wildly,
> I cannot be still;
> for I have heard the sound of the trumpet,
> the alarm of war. (4, 19)

As Yahveh's herald he is obliged to hurl the most terrible threats at Judah. However, by a curious duality, he seems to become both audience and speaker: in the pitiless sentence his mouth utters; he hears with agonized heart his own condemnation:

> If you do not listen to this,
> I will weep in secret for your pride;
> my eyes will run with tears,
> for the Lord's flock is led away to exile. (13, 17)

While interpreting the anguish of Israel, which at the same time is his own, he finds it quite natural to act the part of intercessor. This had been done to some extent by his predecessors, but never so completely or so constantly. This was so apparent that it was to him, the acknowledged advocate of Israel, that the kings unmindful of their ancient privilege, spontaneously turned. Zedekiah, a descendant of David, Solomon, Jehoshaphat and Hezekiah, does not find it strange to go to him in order to beg for his intercession with Yahveh:

Pray to Yahveh our God for us. (37, 3)

In the same way, Jeremiah himself considers the duty of intercession inherent in his mission:

Remember that I stood before you
to speak in their behalf,
to turn away your wrath from them. (18, 20)

Even when he finds this duty distasteful he still performs it:

Tell me, Lord, have I not served you well?
Have I not interceded with you for my enemies
in the time of their misfortune and anguish? (15, 11)

And though Yahveh insists that henceforth all pleading is useless, he still continues to plead:

You, now, do not intercede for this people;
raise not in their behalf a pleading prayer!
Do not urge me, for I will not listen to you. (7, 16)

While Jeremiah intercedes for Israel as if he were king, like a king he is also the leader to be followed, for he has been consecrated by Yahveh himself in the same manner as a king. The formula of consecration is the same as that used for the investiture of the monarch:

Before I formed you in the womb I knew you,
before you were born I dedicated you. (1, 5)

Hence the prophet is to lead his people under God's guidance, and the people are to keep their eyes fixed on their leader:

They shall turn to you,
but you shall not turn to them. (15, 19)

He receives this twofold royal mission in such a way that he cannot refuse it or escape from it, whatever suffering it may entail. Just as the king was one with his people, so Jeremiah's destiny was so completely united to Israel's that he was to share all their trials, death included.

Thus the prophet and Israel are now one and the same. He is one with the Israel of history with whom he identifies himself while remaining personally faithful to Yahveh, and with the future Israel whose coming he is to prepare, or rather which is to begin with him and in him. He is Israel in the melting pot.

✿ ✿ ✿

We come now to examine the unique and exceptional nature of Jeremiah's vocation. He is placed at the spiritual center of Israel for a special reason: so that the New Covenant may be tested and tried out in him.

It would be a great mistake to see in the prophet of a personal religion, the innovator of a religious anarchy in which the individual responds to God's advances in his own way and according to his particular gifts or inspiration. Jeremiah's experience from the beginning of his mission to his death in Egypt was to be a *pilot experience* which would serve for the whole people, to help them along the path to the great Covenant following behind him. It was necessary that he should become the leaven of the new Israel for the establishment of interior religion in which individuals as such would joyfully accept the guidance of God's hand so that His design might be accomplished.

Jeremiah is first of all summoned to begin again in his own

person the spiritual journey of the chosen people, not as they had done it but as they ought to have. To remain under God's hand, Israel needed to give her consent to following the still obscure path along which Yahveh was leading her. As impenetrable as the mystery of God's transcendence is the impossibility of mortal mind to understand His design until He himself provides an explanation, and He does not explain to those who are as yet incapable of understanding. Yahveh's definition of himself, according to one of the traditions of the Pentateuch, is "*I am who am.*" Hence, all that man could do was to advance obediently towards a future that could only be glimpsed confusedly through the threatenings and promises of the prophets. What was essential was that he should not stop on the way.

The endless marches through the desert had more than once discouraged the young nation, but they had still managed to enter the Promised Land. Despite early successes the conquest of Canaan had soon proved to be a difficult task, yet it was brought to an end in a century and a half and the tribes united into a single people in spite of the forces that made for division and tribal independence. When the schism came, it seemed to be about to jeopardize the work of unification accomplished by David and Solomon, and Canaanite infiltration appeared to be seriously threatening the purity of Yahvistic religion. Yet when the moment came, Yahveh raised up men like Jehoshaphat, Hezekiah and Josiah, not to speak of the prophets, to safeguard his work and even to advance it, in spite of the waywardness of a stiff-necked people. Though wars and internal strife still continued, the chosen people could consider that they were now definitely settled in the land which had been promised and given to them. But they would have to leave behind this time of ease—it had been of little advantage to them anyway—for there was no avoiding the great empires that were on the rise. At a later date, in the time of the sages religion was to seem firmly established, but would yet have to be preserved from the influence of Hellenistic thought.

Through all these stages in the history of Israel the patient hand of God can be seen wondrously at work. It is continual exodus with a definite aim, even though it may not apparent, a long journey leading gradually to the peerless figure of the One who was to come in order to fulfill and perfect all things; an exodus in which many of the weaker ones would fall by the wayside, but the strong, the true faithful ones, would continue to advance and after the fall of Jerusalem be gathered into "the remnant."

In this scheme of things Jeremiah occupies a position of first-rate importance. Like the others he has to walk straight on without understanding and with no time for resting. The curt reply of Yahveh to Baruch who, like his master, complains that there is never any respite is:

What I have built, I am tearing down;
what I have planted, I am uprooting:
even the whole land. And do you seek great things for
yourself? Seek them not! I am bringing evil on all
mankind. (45, 4-5)

The farther the prophet advances, the greater become Yahveh's demands on him. It is useless for him to wish to halt. Yahveh only replies by imposing new efforts on him:

If running against men has wearied you,
how will you race against horses?
And if in a land of peace you fall headlong,
what will you do in the thickets of the Jordan? (12, 5)

As in the time of Amos, the prophet is not allowed to make a halt or settle in any place. The hard law imposed by the march forward is that of being converted—a conversion without reservations in which it is useless to look back at the path already trodden when the only important thing is to think of the stages ahead, under penalty of losing God's hand:

If you repent, so that I restore you,
in my presence you shall stand.
If you bring forth the precious without the vile,
you shall be my mouthpiece. (15, 19)

We can imagine the great faith the prophet placed in Yahveh in order not to fall by the way when in his short life he had to travel the long journey that Israel was traveling so slowly and painfully precisely through lack of faith. The faith demanded of him was a heroic one, that already preached by Isaiah during the invasion of Sennacherib when he denounced those who would put their trust and hope elsewhere than in Yahveh.

How had the chosen people dared to throw away their faith when Yahveh, from the first moment he brought them out of Egypt, had never ceased to show proof of his protection and paternal care in the most evident manner? Israel's grievous sin lay precisely in their refusal to cooperate with God.

Like Israel, Jeremiah had been chosen, but he would never forget the fact. How could he not remember it? His mission had been clearly given him by Yahveh:

A prophet to the nations I appointed you. (1, 5)

Yahveh himself would tell him what he was to say:

See, I place my words in your mouth! (1, 9)

Jeremiah's role would be to repeat His messages faithfully:

To whomever I send you, you shall go;
Whatever I command you, you shall speak. (1, 7)

And to reassure the prophet Yahveh multiplies his promises of protection. He will never for a moment desert his messenger:

I am with you to deliver you. (1, 8; cf. 1, 19)

Strong in his faith in God the prophet will be invulnerable:

It is I this day who have made you
    a fortified city,
    a pillar of iron,
    a wall of brass,
against the whole land:
against Judah's kings and princes,
    against its priests and people. (1, 18; cf. 15, 20)

Whatever happens, he will have nothing to fear from anyone. When the enemies of the word rise up against him, He will reduce them to impotence as He had overthrown the nations before Israel:

Yahveh is with me, like a mighty champion:
my persecutors will stumble, they will not triumph. (20, 11)

His victory is assured, as Israel's would have been had they remained faithful:

Though they fight against you,
they shall not prevail,
for I am with you,
to deliver and rescue you. (15, 20)

But his faith, so strongly sustained, must not fail in the least, for Yahveh would abandon his prophet as he had repudiated Israel:

Be not dismayed at them,
lest I dismay you before them.

These imperious commands are addressed to a man who is fainthearted and probably more of a coward than most. Yahveh will support his prophet but will not take his place, like the gods of mythology who are anxious to preserve their heroes. He provides his champion with the most powerful weapons, but leaves to him the ability to make use of them. For God's experiment to acquire its full significance, the one chosen had to be an ordinary man like anyone else. Thus we witness a struggle between Jeremiah and his own nature which was to be a cause of great suffering but also of merit in the triumph over weakness.

His first reaction to Yahveh's summons is one of consternation and refusal. Like Moses, he is astonished at having been chosen and objects:

I do not know how to speak, for I am only a youth. (1, 6)

If anything, he is slow-witted. He allows Hananiah to take the symbolic yoke from his neck without resistance or protest. It is only after an interval of time that, at God's order, he hurls his terrible invective against the false prophet (28, 12-17). When, after the murder of Gedaliah, the army leaders come to him to ask what Yahveh's will is, he does not know what to answer and takes ten days to formulate a judgment of condemnation of which he must have already been aware (42, 7-22).

But there was a greater defect than this. The man whose destiny was to fight to the bitter end was by nature timid and sensitive. He was inclined to mildness, was at ease only in quiet and pleasant company, and felt the need of an atmosphere of sympathy and affection. The harshness of the messages he had to communicate to a people to whom he was bound by ties of fellowship left him grieved and distraught:

> Oh, that my head were a spring of water,
> my eyes a fountain of tears,
> that I might weep day and night
> over the slain of the daughter of my people! (8, 23)

His mission is a continual cause of suffering to him. How can he reconcile loyalty to his country with loyalty to Yahveh? He is inwardly torn by both sentiments and would sacrifice neither:

> Why is my pain continuous,
> my wound incurable? (15, 18)

His role of intercessor is far from an easy one. He has to try and find a way of placating Yahveh when Israel is the personification of rebellion and steadily going from bad to worse while refusing to listen to him. The only result of all his efforts to accomplish his task is rebuff and insult:

> Why did I come forth from the womb,
> to see sorrow and pain,
> to end my days in shame? (20, 18)

This is no exaggeration due to over-sensitiveness, but stark reality which is made all the more unbearable by his susceptible nature:

> But I was like a gentle lamb that is led to the slaughter,
> and I did not know what they had devised against me.
> (11, 19)

Historical evidence confirms the fact that his sufferings were not imaginary—imprisonment, the stocks, the throwing into a cistern, the various attempts on his life. These were only bodily

trials, but what shall be said of those of the heart? What grieves
him above all is that he feels himself part of this sinful world and
can do nothing to save it—part of it because by vocation he is
Israel's heart, and because, though himself guiltless, he is condemned to share the lot of the guilty.

By mistake he is carried away in chains along with the other
prisoners being deported to Babylon, but Babylon is not meant
for him. He would have found peace and safety there, among
"the remnant," the hope for the future. He is set free by
Nebuchadnezzar's officer, Nebuzaradan, and led back by Yahveh
to the dying people to be bound more closely to them. Jehohanan,
the son of Karean, compels him to flee with him into Egypt. This
time probably he was not in chains, but the chains of his
servitude were heavier than those from which he was freed at
Rama. The symbolism is cruelly eloquent, for he can no longer
escape from violence with which others decide his fate, nor from
sharing in the fate of a world that is in its death throes. The
comparison is evident with Christ condemned to share the fate
of a sinful world.

We can understand and excuse him when he longs to put an
end to a life of torment that binds him relentlessly to a cankered
nation from whom his faith and fidelity have now severed him:

> Would that I had in the desert
> a travelers' lodge!
> That I might leave my people
> and depart from them.
> They are all adulterers,
> a faithless band. (9, 1)

In the nightmare of his anguish Yahveh demands from him
such superhuman faith that an excuse can be found for his failings. The cry that is wrung from him is less a sign of revolt than
a confession of weakness:

I will not mention him,
I will speak in his name no more. (20, 9)

Christ in Gethsemani also implored that the chalice might be taken away from him. But for Jeremiah there can be no escape from the hand of Yahveh.

You were too strong for me and you triumphed. (20, 7)

The call he has received cannot be forgotten:

Before you were born I dedicated you. (1, 5)

This dedication was meant specially to give him a new heart, and so it is that the long struggle ends with the victory over self which is Yahveh's victory over him. When we think of all that he had to contend with we cannot but be filled with admiration at his fervent cry:

You, O Lord, know me, you see me,
you have found that at heart I am with you. (12, 3)

Or when he murmurs in the fullness of love:

It is you who are my hope. (17, 14)

Or when above the tumult of the world and the clamor of his enemies we find him listening eagerly to the voice of eternal truth:

When I found your words I devoured them;
they became my joy and the happiness of my heart. (15, 16)

The emphasis is always on the heart, the heart that Yahveh had given him to be offered back whole and entire.

The road that Israel was unable to follow, the road at once so simple and so difficult that leads every man to God, was the same road along which, in spite of natural repugnance and occasional failure, Jeremiah advanced heroically with a confidence born of faith and thus became a man such as God wished. God's experiment could now go on.

On the one hand, Jeremiah is inseparable from the old Israel in that the justice of God seems to demand a reckoning from him for their evil ways as if he himself were responsible. On the other hand, Yahveh isolates him from them in order to show him a new religious attitude. The virgin land he is to enter must be explored by him alone.

The reason for this isolation is the very fact that he has been chosen. To be chosen necessarily demands separation. This law, which applied to Israel, is much more so for Jeremiah, in that he is the link between a world in decline and a world being born. The Israel of the Old Covenant has already passed away.

Of his own accord Jeremiah, too, goes into isolation:

Under the weight of your hand I sat alone. (15, 17)

He is fleeing from a perverse generation whose unconcern and irresponsible indifference he can no longer continue to share:

I did not sit celebrating
in the circle of merrymakers. (15, 17)

Though doomed to the same fate as Israel, he has yet been warned by Yahveh not to share in their joys or sorrows. What would it avail to share in them when the specter of death is standing behind a people filled with the pride of life? What use is it to enter a house of mourning when Yahveh has taken His peace, His loving kindness and His tender mercies away from Israel? What is the use of going into a house of feasting when Yahveh will cause to cease "the voice of mirth and the voice of gladness?" (16, 9). What is the use of having a wife and having sons or daughters when they "shall die of grievous deaths, they shall not be lamented, neither shall they be buried"? (16, 4).

What holds him apart from Judah is also anger—the wrath of Yahveh that boils inside him:

> My wrath brims up within me,
> I am weary of holding it in. (6, 11)

At times he really hates—hate is akin to love—this people that is incapable of receiving the word of salvation. Yahveh had in fact warned him:

> When you speak all these words to them,
> they will not listen to you either;
> when they call to you, you will not answer them.
> ... Faithfulness has disappeared;
> the word itself is banished from their speech. (7, 27-28)

He cannot help feeling repugnance for those who can repay such great love only with the blackest ingratitude:

> Must good be repaid with evil? (18, 20)

The isolation that Yahveh imposes on him and which he himself seeks in order to remain faithful to his God is also a result of his countrymen's attitude. They ask sceptically, "Where is the word of Yahveh?" (17, 15), and his gravest warnings are treated lightly:

> See, the word of Yahveh has become for them an object of scorn. (6, 10)

He himself has become a laughing stock, which in the East

is the worst thing that can happen to a man. To be laughed at
is as good as being an outcast from society:

The word of Yahveh has brought me derision all the day.
(20, 8)

Worse still, the word of life and love that he scatters abroad
brings only hate and discord in its train, and he is the first to
suffer from it:

Woe to me, mother, that you gave me birth!
a man of strife and contention to all the land!
. . . all curse me. (15, 10)

Even his friends have turned against him:

All those who were my friends
are on the watch for any misstep of mine. (20, 10)

His very family is disloyal to him:

Even your brothers, the members of your father's house,
betray you;
they cry out after you with full voice. (12, 6)

Jeremiah treads in solitude the path to where God awaits
him, a solitude of fidelity and desperate courage, full of dis-
illusion, sorrow and anguish.

*   *   *

Spurned by all and feeling that his mission has made him
a misfit, he has no other choice but to turn to his guide. There
is nowhere he can find comfort and consolation or satisfy his
need for tenderness except in Him who already fills his heart.

He is thrown into God's arms by the isolation which he feels so cruelly. It is there that the divine experiment will be completed.

He has no other confidant but God. The dialogue with the Most High leads him to a direct and living experience of that personal worship which until now he knew only theoretically.

It had been good to pray to the Temple as a member of the community, when the children of Israel gathered together in the presence of God to worship Him with the pomp of sacred rites and the sound of music and chanting. But now Jeremiah was banned from the Temple for having dared to announce that Yahveh would treat His house as He had treated Shiloh (7, 12; 26, 6). So he is cut off from the ceremonies and the prayer of the liturgy he loved so much.

In these circumstances it is not surprising he should rely on memory to find food for prayer in the stereotyped phrases he had so often heard. Thus, oddly enough, he takes over the prayer used by the sick asking God to deliver them from the evil spirit they believed possessed them:

Heal me, Yahveh, that I may be healed;
save me that I may be saved. (17, 14)

To describe the anguish he feels in persecution, he borrows the worn-out image of the pit into which the just man's enemy plots to make him fall:

They dig a pit to take my life. (18, 20)

Or that of the net spread treacherously in his path:

They have hid snares for my feet. (18, 22)

He curses his enemies in terms much the same as those used

in witchcraft for laying a curse on an enemy to reduce him to impotence:

So now, deliver their children to famine,
do away with them by the sword.
Let their wives be made childless and widows. (18, 21)

To assert his own faith and hope he takes on a sapiential tone:

Blessed is the man who trusts in Yahveh,
whose hope is Yahveh. (17, 7)

And when he praises Yahveh he sings to himself the *tôda,*
the thanksgiving that those delivered from evil sang at the altar:

Sing to Yahveh,
praise Yahveh,
for he has rescued the life of the poor
from the power of the wicked. (20, 13)

The great dialogue, as can be seen, begins humbly enough. It reminds us of some simple soul who, having forgotten God after childhood, is driven by some present need to seek Him again, and from memory, or while turning over the pages of an old prayer book, recollects old formulas of prayer which he adapts awkwardly to his particular case. They may bring a smile to the lips, but his stammerings, though poor in expression, are heard by God who sees the intention behind them. Jeremiah certainly had never forgotten God, but he was trying to find what nobody had been able to teach him. He was seeking the right words to express his desire for union with God. Like any sincere search for true expression, his groping attempts are deeply moving, and sooner or later were bound to result in less conventional terms with a man so personal in his way of thinking and so intense in feeling as he was. Little by little the prophet's lamentations lose all trace of what Plato in imaginative language calls Κατα- πεπλουμέναι formulas. His language becomes personal and direct, the style sure and robust, the dialogue purer and more vigorous. The words spring from his own consciousness:

You duped me, Yahveh, and I let myself be duped. (20, 7)

The great problem of retribution, which was to be the theme of the Book of Job, is posed by him in terms which, though simple, are sufficient to express his inner anxiety:

You would be in the right, Yahveh,
if I should dispute with you;
even so, I must discuss the case with you:
Why does the way of the godless prosper? (12, 1)

There is deep pathos in his question to Yahveh:

Why is my pain continuous,
my wound incurable, refusing to be healed?
You have indeed become for me a treacherous brook,
whose waters cannot be trusted. (15, 18)

Or when he reminds Yahveh that his sufferings are for His sake:

Know that for you I have borne insult. (15, 15)

We are far from hackneyed formulas here, or where he humbly intercedes for his erring countrymen.

You know, O Lord,
that man is not master of his way;

man's course is not within his choice,
nor is it for him to direct his step.
Punish us, O Lord, but with equity,
not in anger, lest you have us dwindle away. (10, 23-24)

Jeremiah's style has none of the brilliance or passionate vehemence of Job. The purely literary qualities are of secondary importance, but the expression is a truly personal one and that is what counts. He has been able to reject clumsy borrowings and acquire the spontaneity that allows heart-to-heart dialogue with God. For the first time there is an outpouring of interior prayer. Unwitnessed by anybody, it wells up from the soul and rises with simplicity and sincerity towards God at the moment He awaited it.

*   *   *

The great experiment had thus succeeded, as far as it was possible to do so. Yahveh had not yet reached the point of taking possession of man's heart, his chosen one had responded to the call by throwing open his. The new man is born with whom God will make a covenant. This new man, the prototype of future mankind, has created a language capable of responding to the word of Love which, in the striking expression of Jean de Yépès, is uttered in silence and eternally.

The experiment succeeds so well that, until this dawn gives place to the Day, the *anawim,* Jeremiah's direct descendants, will know how to seek God and how to speak to him. On that day perfect Love, abandoning eternity to enter time and leave on it the impress of his triumphal sacrifice, will be able to establish the new people, the true Israel of the Promise, the Church, of which he will be head and heart for ever.

For his power of imagination, energy of expression and magnificence of style. Isaiah stands out among all Old Testament writers with the possible exception of Job. Jeremiah may be inferior to him in literary value, but he has the unquestioned and exceptional merit of having shown that God expects man to adhere to Him in heart completely, unconditionally and lastingly, thus enabling the human person to expand in a purely spiritual climate free from coercion on the part of society.

Any religious system, in fact, which does not insist on the conversion of the heart, even though creating a community of believers, prevents a full development of the soul because it "depersonalizes" it. When social pressure is added to this, individual belief narrows down to a kind of blind fanaticism. Prayer can never rid itself of spectacular gesture, the value of which is overestimated, for the object of prayer is not to witness to one's faith before men but to stand before God without witnesses.

It was thanks to Jeremiah that the world was able henceforth to know the secret heart-to-heart talk with God without the interposition of any creature—the same prayer that Christ was to insist on:

> When you pray, go into your room, and shut the door and pray to you Father who is in secret. (Matt. 6, 6)

Though reserving Jeremiah for Himself, Yahveh had appointed him
> to root up and to tear down,
> to build and to plant. (1, 10)

That only future ages would reveal what he really built and planted is not surprising. When Christ died on the Cross neither the Jews nor the apostles or disciples were able to comprehend the infinite repercussions of his death, which was nothing but a shameful one to their eyes filled with hate or sorrow. Dereliction is the inevitable setting for those events which give birth to the

divine in this world. Jeremiah was the father of a new community after a life of apparent failure, just as Christ, of whom
he is the most recognizable figure, brought to birth in his blood
the Church, the new Israel. It is in the isolation of the Cross,
as St. Paul maintains, that the drama of Israel is transposed and
enlarged to world dimensions.

EZEKIEL

7 Like Jeremiah, Ezekiel was of the priestly race, but of a family, the Ben Sadoc, which probably ministered in Jerusalem. He was deported with King Jehoiachin (Jeconiah) and the flower of the nation after the capture of the city by Nebuchadnezzar in 597. He lived at first at some point on the river Chebar, a tributary of the Euphrates, which flowed through the ancient town of Nippur. It was here in 593 that he had the vision which marked the beginning of his prophetic mission.

In the last few years attempts have been made by biblical scholars to identify Jerusalem as the scene of part of Ezekiel's activity. Recent studies, however, would seem to prove that there are no grounds for accepting this hypothesis or abandoning the traditional position.

Up to the final destruction of the Holy City Ezekiel continued the work of Jeremiah among the exiles, announcing the end of the Old Covenant and the destruction of Zion and her Temple. From 586 on there was a change in his message in that he proclaimed the restoration to be at hand. He describes the history of it beforehand and in a great *tôrah* lays down its social and especially religious organization in order to keep this new Israel free from contamination.

6

A.—A DEFINITE BREAK WITH THE PAST

Jeremiah had announced the end of the Covenant made on Sinai and of all that formed the old Israel—the Davidic monarchy, the Holy City and Temple. Beyond this death, however, he saw the dawn of a resurrection, a New Covenant based on the adhesion of man's heart. But just as Moses was condemned to see the Promised Land from afar without entering it, so Jeremiah was not allowed to see the fulfillment of the Promise. Only the exiles of Babylon would be the men of the future: this he had affirmed time and time again. He himself was to remain in Jerusalem with Zedekiah and end his days in Egypt with that portion of the people whom he had condemned outright. He was never to dissociate himself from the sinful world whose ruin he had foretold. The prophet's personal experience, foreshadowing that of Christ, might have let it be thought that it would not be long before the New Covenant came into being.

What was born, however, from the upheaval of 587 was not the Gospel but *Judaism*. Another five centuries of slow maturation was necessary before Jeremiah's message could find its perfect fulfillment. In this long period of time a new people of God was being formed, different from the old Israel yet only a rough approximation to the ideal. It was transitory stage which would give the Sages time to prepare the mind of man to accept a religion "in spirit and in truth." A new prophet was to arise from the exile where Israel was being reborn. His mission was not to fulfill Jeremiah's message, but to adapt it to the immediate actual situation. This prophet was a priest, deported to Babylon in 598, and in him we can recognize the father of Judaism and the originator of an economy which, though new, was destined to be an economy of transition.

Ezekiel's first task was to direct the minds of the exiles definitely towards the future. They had to be freed from the temptation to look back to the Jerusalem in which, after the siege of 598 and the first mass deportation, Zedekiah continued to reign

with an unexperienced administration (the country had been deprived of its ruling class) over a people enfeebled in the highest
degree. However slight the chances of escaping from the power
of Nabuchadnezzar, there were not wanting obstinate patriots,
especially among the aristocracy, who hoped against hope in a
restoration of David's kingdom in all its former glory. Despite
Jeremiah's warnings, the most fantastic rumors were current
among the exiles and, against the evidence of the facts, were
eagerly believed by those who were ready to cling on to anything
which would save them from despair. Like all the prophets, Ezekiel had to fight against a current of popular opinion and against
the combined energies of a people determined not to disappear.
Like Jeremiah he is resolved to stand firm and has been given
the strength to do so by Yahveh:

> I will make your face as hard as theirs, and your brow as
> stubborn as theirs, like a diamond, harder than flint. Fear
> them not, nor be dismayed at their looks, for they are a re-
> bellious house. (3, 8-9)

Yahveh's assistance was all the more necessary in that in the
midst of the patriotic exaltation of a distressed people, he was
bound, again like Jeremiah, to be regarded as a traitor and de-
featist when he preached the need for a complete break with
the past.

He experienced another difficulty, however, which was unknown to Jeremiah, at least during the early stages of his ministry. Though refusing like his predecessors to belong to the body
of professional prophets, Jeremiah used the same formal language as they, intervening during the religious ceremonies in the
Temple and addressing the people in the great popular gatherings. But in Babylon, far from the Temple, in what manner and
by what sign could Ezekiel get the divine origin of his message
recognized? Was a communication from the God of Israel pos-

sible or even imaginable outside the boundaries of Palestine?

What was to draw the attention of the exiles to Ezekiel was the extraordinary phenomena which accompanied his activity and the oddities of his way of life. His paralysis, his dumbness, his fainting fits, all these strange manifestations appeared providential and convinced his hearers that he was possessed by the spirit of Yahveh:

> And the spirit lifted me up and seized me.
> And I went away, my heart full of bitterness and indignation, while the hand of Yahveh rested heavily upon me. (3, 14)

It was believed that diseases, and especially psychic disturbances, were due to the work of a *daimon*. The various infirmities to which the prophet was subject and the unusualness of his ordinary behavior were more than sufficient to create an impression on those who came in contact with him, and inspire them with reverential silence. The fact that we find the "elders" seeking him out and asking his advice is a proof that they discerned in him the presence of a mysterious force and believed the spirit of Yahveh to be dwelling in him. He was therefore listened to with attention and became a figure in the public eye and a subject of discussion among all the Jews scattered through Babylonia. The report of his visions and his oracles was passed from town to town, and thus though far from the Temple, he was able to gain the confidence of his fellow-countrymen.

The prophet sets about destroying one after the other the illusions that would hinder his constructive mission.

The City, ever present in their thoughts, which it is unnecessary even to name:

> If I forget you, Jerusalem,
> may my right hand be forgotten!
> May my tongue cleave to my palate
> if I remember you not. (Ps. 137, 5-6)

After hesitating whether to march on Jerusalem or the Ammonite capital, Nebuchadnezzar was led by God to attack Judah's stronghold. The destruction of the city had begun. Sitting at a street corner, it may be, Ezekiel describes the operations of the siege in mime:

Take a clay tablet; lay it in front of you, and draw on it a city (Jerusalem). Raise a siege against it; build a tower, lay out a ramp, pitch camps and set up battering rams all around. Then take an iron griddle and set it up as an iron wall between you and the city. . . . This shall be a sign for the house of Israel. (4, 1-3)

In the manner of the inhabitants of a besieged town he measures out a scanty ration of water and ersatz bread (4, 9-11). His audience is thus able to see clearly the fate of Jerusalem:

I am destroying the supply of bread in Jerusalem. They shall eat bread which they have weighed out anxiously, and they shall drink water which they have measured out fearfully, so that, owing to the scarcity of bread and water, everyone shall be filled with terror and waste away because of his sins.
(4, 16-17)

The end of the siege is shown just as forcibly. He shaves his head and beard with a razor and divides the hair into three parts —one for the fire, another for the sword, and a third for the wind:

A third of your people shall die of pestilence and perish of hunger, another third shall fall by the sword, and a third I will scatter in every direction, and I will pursue them with the sword. (5, 12)

The dynasty of David: to hope in its continuance is just as vain. Zedekiah may well continue to put up a show of confidence, engage in diplomatic intrigues and try to revive former coalitions against Babylon, but it is only the old played-out game and a short-sighted policy that will lead to fresh disaster. And anyway, who is this man put on the throne of David by Nebuchadnezzar in place of his nephew Jehoiachin? Ezekiel cannot recognize him as the legitimate king. The dynasty has ceased to exist now that Jehoiachin is in exile. Moreover, as he is a vassal of the king of Babylon, Zedekiah would only perjure himself if he broke the covenant which binds him, not to Yahveh as in the case of his predecessors, but to Babylon:

> In the home of the king who set him up to rule, whose oath he spurned, whose covenant with him he broke, there in Babylon I swear he shall die. (17, 16)

It is useless for him to claim to rule the country as David's successor. He will not escape the fate of the condemned people, nor that of his brother Jehoahaz who after the death of Josiah was exiled to Egypt (19, 5-9). One night Ezekiel gathers together his possessions, makes a hole in the earthen wall of his house and goes out into the dark:

> I am a sign for you: as I have done, so shall it be done to them; as captives they shall go into exile. The prince who is among them shall shoulder his burden and set out in darkness, going through a hole that he has dug in the wall, and covering his face lest he be seen by anyone. (12, 11-12)

Finally, there is the Temple. Around it all illusions crystalize; its inviolability was affirmed by Isaiah and denied by Jeremiah, yet in it resided Yahveh's glory and, as long as it remained on top of Zion, it would keep Israel alive. In the shadow of this divine protection Israel feels safe:

"Shall we not," they say, "be building houses soon?
The city is the kettle, and we are the meat." (11, 3)

While he is seated in the midst of the elders of Israel exiled in Babylon, Ezekiel falls into an ecstasy. Rapt in spirit he traverses frontiers and countries and arrives at the House of Yahveh from the north, the traditional invasion route. He enters the gates and passes through the walls, and is horrified to find monstrous idols to which sacrifices are being offered, while the women sit and bewail the death of Tammuz just as in Babylon. The Temple is profaned and Yahveh is abandoning his sanctuary. Driven out by Israel's sin, he withdraws by the eastern gate.

And the glory of Yahveh went up from the midst of the city, and stood upon the mountain which is on the east side of the city. (11, 23)

Returning to himself, the prophet relates his vision to those around him (11, 25). There is no further hope in the Temple that is now empty of Yahveh's glory.

While averting their gaze from a past that is sinking to its death, the exiles will not even have the bitter consolation of being able to mourn for what was the pride of their greatness, the joy of their eyes, the passion of their souls (24, 21-23). On his wife's death the prophet is forbidden to go into mourning, another behavior which could not fail to focus attention on him. To leave no room for misunderstanding he explains the reason:

You shall do as I have done, not covering your beards nor eating the customary bread. Your turbans shall remain on your heads, your sandals on your feet. You shall not mourn or weep. (24, 22-23)

This entirely corrupt world in which there is nothing worth

saving does not deserve a farewell gesture or a word of regret. The "kettle" in which those in Judah thought themselves safe is corroded with rust:

> Then I will set it empty on the coals,
> till its metal glows red hot,
> till the impurities in it melt,
> and its rust disappears.
> Yet not even with fire will its great rust be removed . . .
> therefore you shall not be purified
> until I wreak my fury on you. (24, 11-13)

The curse is more than justified by the utter defilement of the country. The blood that has been shed has been left uncovered and cries out for vengeance. The whole land is profaned even to the courts of the Temple (9, 7). The unclean soil must be cleared; mountains, hills and valleys will vomit their inhabitants.

The last prophet of disaster, Ezekiel sweeps away the past before opening up prospects of restoration on which the thoughts of Israel will henceforth turn. Those remaining in Judea repeat in vain:

> Abraham, though but a single individual, received possession of the land; we, therefore, being many, have as permanent possession the land that has been given to us. (33, 24)

Nothing of what remains there will be restored. Yahveh will rebuild only on ruins and with new materials.

It is noteworthy that *each new stage in the spiritual life requires a complete break with the past,* and this break does not allow of regrets and farewells. The hand of God guides towards a future the consistent feature of which is newness. Abraham leaves his own country forever to enter that of the Promise. Christ's disciples leave all to follow the Master. Saul, the un-

compromising Pharisee, starts life anew to become the apostle
of the one he was persecuting:
  No one, having put his hand to the plow and looking back, is
  fit for the kingdom of God. (Lk. 9, 62).

B.—THE NEW WORLD IN OUTLINE

  Ezekiel's zeal in destroying the illusions of the exiles is explained by the mission he had received. This was a positive one,
consisting in the use of them as the raw material for a first attempt at the creation of a new world. He could look nowhere
but ahead if he were not to betray the responsibilities that were
laid on him.
  But would not the Jews in Babylon, whose eyes he was trying
to turn away from a dead past, be tempted to think themselves
completely cut off from the religion of Israel and its laws, and
be ready to lose their identity by disappearing into the people
among whom they were forcibly settled as the ten tribes had
done after the fall of Samaria? It is precisely against such a counsel of despair that the prophet reacts. When the elders come to
consult him he tells them emphatically:

  When you say:
  "We shall be like the nations, like the peoples of foreign lands,
  serving wood and stone."
  As I live, says the Lord God,
  with a mighty hand and outstretched arm,
  with poured-out wrath, I swear I will be king over you!
                                                  (20, 32-33)

  Woe to those who fall into the idolatry of another people!
(14, 1-11). Not only are the exiles not taken from out God's hand,
they are more firmly established under it than anyone else, for
they are the only true Israel and on them Yahveh intends to
build the restoration of a holy people.

The starting point of this restoration is the prospect of the New Covenant such as Jeremiah had imagined it. He had made the fundamental discovery that the old Israel was corrupt to its very roots, and had been corrupt from the first. Ezekiel affirms the same in his turn:

> By origin and birth you are of the land of Canaan; your father was an Amorite and your mother a Hittite, (16, 3)

Like Jeremiah, Ezekiel has a presentiment of divine grace at the same time as he notes the fact of sin. Yahveh will himself fashion hearts capable of obedience and open to his spirit:

> I will give you a new heart and place a new spirit within you, taking from your bodies your stony hearts and giving you natural hearts.
> I will put my spirit within you and make you live by my statutes. (36, 26-27)

Again like Jeremiah, Ezekiel realizes that, as the law will be engraved on the soul, religion will necessarily become personal and interior, and each one will be able to find God in his heart and will be responsible for his personal fidelity. And Yahveh concludes:

> As for those whose hearts are devoted to their idols and to their detestable abominations, I will bring down their conduct upon their heads. (11, 21)

There is here an obvious similarity between the two prophets, but it goes no farther. Jeremiah's vision is very close to the Gospel, while the sketch Ezekiel produces is only rudimentary and imperfectly faithful to its model. Jeremiah sees further than Ezekiel and his thought is purer, doubtless owing to the fact

that, unlike his successor, he did not have to put his hand to the
actual work of reconstruction. The theorist is in a better position
to keep a doctrine free from compromise than is one who has
to put it into practice. Moreover, before the religion of Israel
could become a religion "in spirit and truth," Jewish thought
needed to grow and mature. Until all was ready for the creation
of a New Covenant that would apply to all mankind there had
to be a transitional period which would provide a temporary
framework within which the idea of a personal religion could
slowly develop. In short, while Jeremiah keeps to the stage of
promises, with Ezekiel the new economy begins to take shape
and is already being tried out on the banks of the Euphrates
among the exiles.

The Judgment of Yahveh will not apply to Babylon as it does
to Zion. It is true that the scribe clothed in linen charged to
execute vengeance in the holy city (9, 4) was to spare those
who mourned for the abominations committed in the Temple,
but Ezekiel thinks that even the just will not be spared in ancient
Jerusalem. All alike who are present there will come under the
same condemnation:

> Thus says the Lord:
> See! I am coming at you;
> I will draw my sword from its sheath
> and cut off from you the virtuous and the wicked. (21, 8)

But as it is from the exiles that the new people will be born,
they will not be condemned or rejected because of the sin of
the community, the sin of their fathers. Yahveh even lets them
become aware of the role they are to play. Salvation is in their
hands, subject to individual righteousness:

> For all lives are mine;
> the life of the father is like the life of the son,
> both are mine; only the one who sins shall die. (18, 4)

Each one, then, must undertake his own responsibilities. No one is now answerable for the salvation of others. Noah, Daniel and Job, the supreme examples of righteous men, can save only themselves by their righteousness. They cannot atone for their country, or even for their sons and daughters (14, 13-20).

These being the characteristics of the new economy of salvation, the prophet's activity begins to take a new direction. God's herald is no longer to scourge the sins of a people, but to point out to each one of them the road to be followed. In any case, it was no longer possible for Ezekiel to address the collectivity as a whole, as in Babylon he had access only to dispersed and isolated groups. Hosea was the sentinel of all Ephraim; Ezekiel is the guard of the individual. He is obliged to be so, for if he fails in his duty, Yahveh is at hand to warn him:

The wicked man shall die for his sin,
but I will hold you responsible for his death. (3, 18; 33, 8)

If, however, he reproves the sinner and he does not turn from his wicked ways, the prophet will not be to blame (33, 9). Conversion is therefore something personal:

As I live, says the Lord God,
I swear I take no pleasure in the death of the wicked man,
but rather in the wicked man's conversion, that he may live.
(33, 11)

A man himself in the last resort must decide on his salvation or damnation, his life or death:

When a virtuous man turns away from what is right and does wrong, he shall die for it. But when a wicked man turns away from wickedness and does what is right and just, because of this he shall live. (33, 18-19)

Analyzing all the possible cases, Ezekiel does his utmost to apply the principle of retribution as rigorously as possible. Like all Jews of his time, he sees nothing beyond the horizons of this world. As for them, for him divine justice operates only here below. He could not therefore avoid the conclusion that happiness is bound up with virtue, and misfortune with wrong-doing. But by transferring to the individual what had applied to the people as a whole, that obedience is a necessary condition of life, he was unwittingly setting a new and grave problem, namely the danger inherent in the transference of Israel's hopes from the collective to the personal sphere. The problem was to prove a difficult one and was to offer the Sages ample matter for reflection. Job's eloquent protest would have its due weight of influence in the debate. On this point, therefore, Ezekiel gives us only an imperfect image of what a personal religion should be.

Another difficulty, perhaps a graver one, was that, while recognizing the need for an interior religion, Ezekiel was unable to free himself from the belief that the divine presence was impossible outside the sanctuary.

Jeremiah had made the discovery that it was possible to pray to Yahveh outside the Temple. His experience could serve as an example to the exiles, and in fact did so. It was possible for them from now on to worship God even when they were far from the land of Palestine. Jeremiah had written as much to the deportees, and Ezekiel repeats the same in Yahveh's name, but adding extremely significant words:

Though I have removed them far among the nations and scattered them far over foreign countries, yet will I be to them *a sanctuary* for *a little while* in the countries to which they have gone. (11, 16)

Thus, while the Temple has no further importance for Jeremiah, Ezekiel's thoughts are never far from a temple—not the old one which will be destroyed, but another which will be rebuilt after the time of trial, and in the meantime a substitute one which he proposes to the exiles for the time being.

It is evident that however personal the religious experience may be, it can never be anarchical. The hand of God draws men together at the same time as it lays hold of them individually. But short of concentrating on the ideal presented by Jeremiah— a purely spiritual experience that was to be realized in Christ— Judaism could do nothing else in order to reach the faithful of the Diaspora except regroup itself round the ancient national structure, retouching it and adapting it as the circumstances demanded. Thus, while not abandoning the idea of the Temple, Ezekiel readjusts it to suit the needs of the new religious life.

To understand the regression of Ezekiel's thought in respect of that of Jeremiah, but also his originality, the significance of the Temple in the religious life of Israel must not be lost sight of. Isaiah had shown Yahveh as the God of Heaven, seated over Jerusalem as King, exercising a loving and jealous care for all that happened in Palestine. But like all the gods of the Semitic peoples, Yahveh possessed a place on earth where his foot rested, thus giving concreteness to his presence among his people. This place was the Temple. Temple and Heaven were two closely connected realities. "Yahveh's sanctuary" applied equally to both. In other words, the Temple was Heaven coming down to touch earth. The Ark was Yahveh's pedestal and was associated with the firmament, the celestial throne of his divinity. The cherubim and everything surrounding the Ark symbolized the clouds and lightning, the celestial attributes of Yahveh.

Ezekiel does not see things differently. In the vision with which the book opens, Yahveh appears over the Ark, all of sapphire like the firmament, while the burning coals flash out and the living creatures, the cherubim, move their wings with thunderous noise:

> In among the living creatures something like burning coals of fire could be seen; they seemed like torches, moving to

and fro among the living creatures. The fire gleamed, and from it came forth flashes of lightning. (1, 13)

Then I heard the sound of their wings. . . . When they moved, the sound of the tumult was like the din of an army. (1, 24)

Above the firmament over their heads, something like a throne could be seen, looking like sapphire. Upon it was seated, up above, one who had the appearance of a man. (1, 26)

Thus for the prophet, Yahveh remains the Uranian, the Heavenly One who lowers the firmament of his throne down to earth in order to declare his presence among men. He sets the soles of his feet in this place of his election (43, 7). The idea is the traditional one, but it needed to be adapted to a new reality. Israel is no longer a group in its own land, but is scattered in exile, and the God of Sinai is turning his face towards a dispersed people.

It is here that the representation of Heaven as Yahveh's habitation begins to be amplified to cover not only the territory of Judah but any part of the world inhabited by the children of Israel. Yahveh's glory will descend from the firmament in every place they are. That is why shortly after Ezekiel the priestly passages of Exodus begin to relate how His glory descended in the desert in every place the Ark rested. While Isaiah had seen Yahveh Sabaoth only in his Temple in Zion, Ezekiel sees this Temple on the banks of the Chebar (1, 3), in the midst of the captives who will thus not be deprived of his presence.

The novelty of Ezekiel's message lies therefore in the fact that *the glory of Yahveh* which fills the immensity of the heavens *can descend simultaneously* in every place that Israel is living. This is the real significance of the prophet's opening vision. The mobility of Yahveh's throne explains the multiplicity of detail with which Ezekiel loads his description. Under the living crea-

tures who support the throne there are wheels—a self-evident
symbol—which advance in all directions according as the spirit
moves them:

> Wherever the spirit wished to go, there the wheels went,
> and they were raised together with the living creatures.
>
> (1, 20)

Borne aloft by the wheeled chariots, the glory of Yahveh
leaves his Temple and comes to rest on the Mount of Olives:

> Then the cherubim lifted their wings,
> and the wheels went along with them,
> while up above them was the glory of the God of Israel.
> And the Glory of Yahveh rose from the city
> and took a stand on the mountain which is to the east of
> the city. (11, 22-23)

However movable it may be, the glory of Yahveh still pre-
serves the Temple of Jerusalem as the normal place of its
presence. His sanctuary among the exiles is only a temporary
one. If Yahveh has left his dwelling place it is because he could
not remain in a place that has been profaned. When the time
comes to return, and the Temple is rebuilt with new stones, he
will enter it in triumph by the eastern gate, which was probably
opened for the ancient processions of the God-King (43, 4).
Thus Yahveh will return to the same place where Isaiah had
seen Him enthroned.

Unlike Isaiah, Ezekiel avoids speaking of Yahveh the King.
Probably the name had too many unpleasant associations, the
sacrifice of the first-born, to take one example. Moreover, the
kingship of Yahveh might seem to require the restoration of
the Davidic monarchy with all its privileges. The prophet does
not want to see a king as the center of the new Israel. A prince

would be sufficient as the guardian of justice, who would be
allowed certain rights of precedence but would be strictly *primus
inter pares* and would not receive a religious consecration. The
new Israel should not be modelled on the old. If it could not be
presented as a pure spiritual experience, at least it would try to
show its theocratic character.

In place of the title of King, Ezekiel prefers that of *Shepherd*.
A traditional title in Babylonia, it was better suited to his message
in the sense that, once having left his Temple, Yahveh would go
about the world seeking his faithful ones to gather them together
again on his holy mountain.

> As a shepherd tends his flock
> when he finds himself among his scattered sheep,
> so will I tend my sheep.
> I will rescue them from every place where they were
> scattered, when it was cloudy and dark. . . .
> I will pasture them upon the mountains of Israel,
> in the land's ravines and all its inhabited places.
> In good pastures will I pasture them, and on the mountain
> heights of Israel shall be their grazing ground. (34, 12-14)

Yahveh will return with his sheep to the mountains of
Palestine which are finally cleansed of all their former abominations:

> I will settle crowds of men upon you, the whole house of
> Israel; cities shall be re-peopled and ruins rebuilt. I will
> settle crowds of men and beasts upon you, to multiply and be
> fruitful. (36, 10-11)

Then the age of universal peace and harmony sung of by
the psalmists and foretold by the prophets will begin as a preparation for the final coming of Yahveh the King:

I, Yahveh, will be their God, and my servant David shall be
prince among them.
I, Yahveh, have spoken.
I will make a covenant of peace with them, and rid the
country of ravenous beasts, that they may dwell securely
in the desert and sleep in the forests. I will place them about
my hill, sending rain in due season, rains that shall be a
blessing to them. (34, 24-26)

The unity of man with the earth will be restored because man
will have found unity with his God:

You shall live in the land I gave your fathers;
you shall be my people, and I will be your God . . .
I will order the grain to be abundant . . . I will increase the
fruit on your trees and the crops in your fields. (36, 28-30)

*   *   *

In some aspects Ezekiel's message is as radical as Jeremiah's.
Like his predecessor he makes a clean sweep of the past. The
broken pieces cannot be mended; there must be a new creation.
Such is the sense of the vision of the dead bones which the
Spirit will clothe again with their flesh and bring to life:

Son of man, these bones are the whole house of Israel. . . .
I will open your graves and have you rise from them. . . .
I will put my spirit in you that you may live, and I will
settle you upon your land. (37, 11-14)

Where death reigned, the spring gushing from the Temple
will bring life:

This water flows into the eastern district,
down upon the Araba, and empties into the sea,
the salt waters, which it makes fresh.

Wherever the river flows, every sort of living creature that
can multiply shall live...
wherever this water comes, the sea shall be made fresh,
and everything shall live wherever the river flows. (47, 8-9)

But where the waters do not flow, there will be death there:

The marshes and swamps shall not be made fresh;
they shall be left for salt. (47, 11)

Still, the way in which the prophet sees the realization of
his message is very far from the purity of Jeremiah's ideal. It is
true that from the interior religion preached by Jeremiah he
adheres to the idea that God's hand is stretched out over all the
dispersed of Israel, but it is around a material center, the
Temple, that he thinks they will be gathered together again.
Yet he is aware of the imperfection of his conception and is con-
tinually correcting it in order to bring it more into line with the
ideal; but despite his power of imagination, he is unable to
translate into concrete terms all the wealth of the divine promises.
Though he stretches his vision to the utmost limits of utopian
fantasy, empties Palestine of all its inhabitants and regroups
the twelve tribes of Israel in order of hierarchy and dignity in
a country which, from afar, appears as a mountain from which
the valleys have disappeared, yet he still remains dissatisfied.
    It is obvious that the new Israel whose religion was to be
interior and personal could not be the one Ezekiel was called
upon to reconstruct, nor is it possible to imagine a completely
pure world in which men still retain their freedom to do evil.
Splendid as it is, his conception remains a long way behind what
God himself would one day offer to mankind. The idea formed
by a human mind can never approach the stupendous reality
of what God has reserved for us. Between our hopes and his
fulfillment of them there is a gap that can never be bridged by
human imagination, even though inspired by the Holy Spirit.

Like his predecessors, and like ourselves as well, when it is a question of preparing on earth the coming of the kingdom of God, the work done by Ezekiel could only be provisional. Let us reflect that, like this great prophet, we should never feel satisfied with the attempts we make, never consider final or lasting what Christianity has constructed in the course of time. However wise and prudent our plans may be, they are only childish designs compared with God's designs. From it they may draw inspiration, but its harmony and perfection will always escape us until the day of its final revelation.

C.—A VISION OF PURITY

The religious restoration that is the work of Ezekiel was in large measure a utopian dream. It was not that he was lacking in realism, but it was impossible for him to introduce the impenetrable design of God into time, and much less bring about its fulfillment.

Throughout the Old Testament we find a thirst and a quest for the infinite defying all possibility of positive, historical fulfillment. Ezekiel's Utopia, common to the rest of the Bible, is based on God's promise which could not be fulfilled by human power. But it has at least a theological value, in the sense that it allows us to understand the general direction of the desires and hopes of Israel, which were to remain unsatisfied till Christ's Church came to fulfill them.

The utopian character of Ezekiel's work is due in great part to his *obsession with purity*, an obsession which can perhaps be attributed to his concern for legalism. This is something of which we are rather shy nowadays. It is evident that from the picture which has been drawn of him, Ezekiel emerges as the father of Judaism, with all his real greatness but also with his narrowness of outlook. The hardening of the mind in later life must not, however, blind us as to the importance of his early intuition. If we do not grasp the positive value of his vision of purity, we will misunderstand the meaning of his message. While Jeremiah was concerned only with the interior drama of Israel, Ezekiel had to take into account a new reality among the dispersed exiles. In order to survive, the Israelites must preserve the characteristics which distinguished them from the peoples around them. To become once again a nation, they must not allow themselves to be assimilated by them and lose their identity. If Yahveh continues to lay his hand upon his scattered people, it is in order to keep them separated and apart from the rest of the world, and one day bring them to a new birth.

There can be no doubt that Ezekiel's priestly origin exercised a decisive influence on his thought. One of the essential tasks of the priest was to see that the laws of *ritual purity* were observed, especially as in the old Jerusalem the priesthood had often failed in this task:

> Her priests violate my law and profane what is holy to me; they do not distinguish between the sacred and the profane, nor teach the difference between the unclean and the clean; they pay no attention to my Sabbaths, so that I have been profaned in their midst. (22, 26)

The prophet had never been wanting in scrupulous fidelity to legal prescription. Even though Yahveh himself bids him partake of unclean food, Ezekiel is ready to protest.

> "Oh no, Lord God!" I protested. "Never have I been made unclean, and from my youth till now, never have I eaten carrion flesh or that torn by wild beasts; never has any unclean meat entered my mouth." (4, 14)

There is nothing surprising in the fact, therefore, that he conceives sin as ritual impurity, even more than do his predecessors. Isaiah symbolized it especially by the shedding of blood,

Jeremiah by uncleanness from contact with the bodies of the
dead. Both these ideas are adopted by Ezekiel. Thus, to describe
the profanation of the holy places he evokes the image of corpses:

Then shall they know that I am Yahveh,
when their slain shall be amid their idols,
all about their altars,
on every high hill and mountain top,
beneath every green tree and leafy oak,
wherever they offered appeasing odors to any of their gods.
(6, 13; cf. 43, 9)

At the ultimate deconsecration of his Temple, Yahveh cries to
the executioners of his justice:

Defile the temple; fill the courts with the slain! (9, 7)

Bloodshed likewise symbolizes sin, but he discards the moral
aspect added to it by Jeremiah, who saw it as a case of *innocent*
blood. Ezekiel confines himself strictly to the feeling of intuitive
repulsion caused by the sight of blood.

Israel is represented by Ezekiel as a woman who has sinned
from birth. He sees her first as newly-born, weltering in her
blood, cast out in the open country as an object of horror. Then
Yahveh intervenes to cleanse her:

Then I bathed you with water and washed away your
blood. (16, 9)

To take away her uncleanness she had to be washed in water
and rubbed with salt (14, 4), probably an allusion to the purification rites practiced in the Temple. These rites come quite
naturally into the prophet's mind when he speaks about the
conversion of his people. In promising to give Israel a new heart,
Yahveh says:

I will sprinkle clean water upon you
to cleanse you from all your impurities,
and from all your idols I will cleanse you. (36, 25)

This is not simply a mode of expression borrowed from
Ezekiel's priestly upbringing. A woman's impurity, for example,
can be regarded as a symbol of Israel's sin.

In my sight their conduct was like the defilement
of a menstrous woman. (36, 17)

But there is much more here than a symbol. To approach a
woman during her menstruation was a crime in itself, not
lesser than any other violation of the moral law, as the following
passage shows:

A man is virtuous,
... if he does not raise his eyes to the idols of
the house of Israel,
if he does not defile his neighbor's wife,
nor have relations with a woman in her menstrual period,
if he oppresses no one,
and gives back the pledge received for a debt.
(18, 5-7; cf. 22, 10)

Obviously, there is here an out-of-date confusion between
morality and ritual purity, and it would seem that there was a
need for further purification of Israel's religion before it could
offer its followers a code of behavior inspired by a purely rational ethic. The fact is that the Bible, while insisting on the moral
side of its teaching, never confined itself to this alone. It also
proposed to impress upon the chosen people—and in a concrete manner—a clear awareness of their having been chosen
and being separated from all the peoples around them. We must
consider this side of the question for an explanation of the
ritualism which is to be found in post-exilic Judaism with a rigor
we might be tempted to judge excessive.

Israel was not to be like the other nations who worshipped wood and stones (20, 32). Though they were living in exile, Yahveh still continues to hold his hand over them so as to make of them a new people. They must conduct themselves according to the law (20, 11). They must observe the Sabbath, and the rest of the world must know it:

Keep holy my Sabbaths, as a sign between me and you,
to show that I am Yahveh, your God. (20, 20)

The exiles will show their fidelity to the Sabbaths as well as to circumcision and other customs of Israel in order to affirm that they belong exclusively to Yahveh. Thus they will be a pure people and Yahveh's own.

Ezekiel's concern for this purity extends to everything that has to do with Israel's destiny. Country and Temple, above all, must be clearly distinguished from all else that exists and be their dominant thought. Jerusalem is seen by Ezekiel from Babylon. The city appears to him from afar, set in the midst of the nations (5, 5). The angle of vision is a new one, for before this no prophet had ever been led to see the Holy Land from the outside. It took the exile to give an awareness of a Zion viewed geographically, surrounded by the rest of the world.

Would Judea, then, be submerged, handed over to strangers and barbarians and utterly profaned (7, 22-24)? or would it not rise up, as a mountain rises above the plain, to receive a holy people, a people set apart by their God? Yahveh replies:

For on my holy mountain, on the mountain height of Israel,
there the whole house of Israel without exception shall
worship me; there I will accept them, and there I will claim
your tributes and the first fruits of your offerings, and
all that you dedicate. As a pleasing odor I will accept

you, when I have brought you from among the nations and
gathered you out of the countries over which you were
scattered; and by means of you I will manifest my
holiness in the sight of the nations. (20, 40-41)

Ezekiel's imagination dwells lovingly on this picture of an
entirely pure world standing out from the rest of the world,
and with everything converging towards the summit that dominates it. A few steps allow the faithful to reach the sacred precinct and enter the outer court through well-guarded gates. A
few more steps lead to the inner court, to which only priests and
Levites have access; even the prince will only have the right
to watch from the doorway. The priests are clothed in sacred
vestments which must be left behind when they leave. The last
steps lead up to the sanctuary properly speaking, the "temple"
taken in its original sense, the place strictly reserved for the
divinity, where Yahveh himself is present (43, 7), behind the
massive wall which no one is to pass except (as he was later
to be called) the High Priest. The whole is formed in a mag-
nificent ascension, in the image of a world raised up by God
from the morass of sin towards the heights where he dwells.

It is Yahveh who from the summit truly takes hold of all
things with the power of his hand, for without his assistance
Israel would fall back into the depths of impurity. If the chosen
people are clothed with the purity which distinguishes them
from the rest of the world, they have no reason to be proud of
the fact. To realize that they owe it to God alone, it is enough
for them to remember the times of their infidelity, of which
Yahveh reminds them:

Through all your abominations and harlotries you
remembered
nothing of when you were a girl, stark naked and weltering
in your blood. (16, 22)

22

Once their sin has been forgiven Israel will still have cause to be ashamed of their past infidelities:

> Then you shall remember your evil conduct, and that your deeds were not good; you shall loathe yourselves for your sins and your abominations. . . . Be ashamed and abashed because of your conduct, O house of Israel. (36, 31-32)

From now on all the feastdays of the community will be accompanied by rites of expiation as a ceaseless reminder that the people ascending the holy mountain are a people that has become pure after being purified.

Israel's separation from the rest of the world would naturally give rise to a temptation to self-complacency and, despite Ezekiel's warnings, to a sense of pride. That they later succumbed to this temptation is only too true, but we must not allow this to detract from the greatness of his message. To entrust oneself to God's hand means to climb the holy mountain and raise oneself up gradually from human baseness without thereby losing sight of past failings. It means also to understand that it is not for the "elect" to come down to the world, but for the world to rise up towards the elect. There is no other way for Christ's Church to draw the world to herself and save it.

D.—YAHVEH'S GLORY THE MAIN DESIRE

Israel's election is therefore confirmed and renewed. Besides the temptation to pride with which Israel might be inspired by this privilege even when fully aware of her disgraceful past and the favor that had been granted her, there was also the danger that God's people might shut themselves up in a narrow puritanism and be drawn towards a self-centered and exclusive way of life without any regard for the rest of the world.

Ezekiel was able to avoid this danger in his message to the exiles. He well realized that Israel's history was not a dead end where everything came to a stop, but an episode in a much wider history of the whole of mankind. If Yahveh intervenes in favor of his people, he does so solely for the glory of his name. It was in order that his name should not be dishonored in the eyes of the nations that he brought Israel out of Egypt and in spite of their acts of rebellion did not exterminate them in the desert (20, 9-14). If he still intends to re-establish them, it is in order that his name may be sanctified, and not because Israel, which is but sin and corruption, has any claim at all on him (20, 44). She has received her privilege only in order to serve Yahveh. From this it follows that she has the heavy responsibility of manifesting the glory of her God to the world.

❉ ❉ ❉

The idea is not new. All the prophets had sought to convince Israel that it was they who owed service to Yahveh, and not Yahveh who was at his people's beck and call. Some of them had still further insisted that if Israel was the object of his free choice, the destiny of the chosen people concerned the rest of the world in one way or another. Especially in Jeremiah we find an awareness that Judah's presence had a bearing on the destiny of the surrounding peoples. Though a witness to Israel's drama from the inside, he had an impression that it was a drama around which the whole world was revolving, and so his message, while addressed to Israel, held good for all peoples. It is enough to remember that when he was ordered to announce the death and restoration of his people, he had from the beginning of his ministry been "set over nations and over kingdoms, to root up and to tear down, to destroy and to demolish" (Jer. 1, 10).

It would be unreasonable to expect a similar depth of understanding from a prophet who is considering events from the outside and, even more, from a foreign land. But though Ezekiel has no concept that Israel may be drawing the world to life or death in her wake, he is better placed to notice the reaction of the gentile nations to the fall of Jerusalem. Like all the other prisoners he had experienced the contempt of the conquerors and the shame of defeat. It is enough to note the insistence with which he speaks of the infamy to which the sinful nation is doomed to hear the echo of his own grief.

It was not alone the patriot that suffered in him. However deep the wound to his national pride, the believer in him was still more grieved at the thought that the catastrophe was a blow to Yahveh's glory:

In you I shall be profaned in the eyes of the nations. (22, 16)

It is inevitable that defeat reflects upon the ideal for which one is fighting. That Yahveh wished to show them that his cause was not tied to theirs was something that could be understood by the Hebrews themselves, but how could the other nations attribute Israel's misfortunes to the vengeance of her God? For her own part, Israel ought not to have the least doubt about the real cause of these misfortunes. The prophets had made the explanation quite clear with their endless threatenings that Yahveh would strike his stiff-necked people hard in order to make them recognize the justice of his hand. Ezekiel, too, is careful not to let them forget this:

They shall know that I, Yahveh, have spoken in my jealousy,
when I spend my fury upon them. (5, 13)

The exiles must not cherish the illusion of seeing their lost homeland in an idyllic light from afar. To preserve them from this and keep them with a clear vision of reality, Yahveh will send to Babylon unimpeachable witnesses who have escaped from the disaster and who will report all the abominations that

Jerusalem continues to persevere in, so that the exiles can make
no mistake about the meaning of the punishment.

> Some survivors shall be left who will bring out sons
> and daughters; when they come out to you, you shall see
> their conduct and actions, for you shall then know that
> it was not without reason that I did to it what I did. (14, 22)

So the exiles must not lament over the fate of the kingdom,
for Yahveh's vengeance is more than justified. But the other
nations must be enlightened in their turn. Yahveh wishes them
to know who it is who has kindled this devouring and unquench-
able fire (21, 4). So to them as well he will send witnesses:

> Yet I will leave a few of them to escape the sword, famine
> and pestilence, so that they may tell of all their abominations
> among the nations to which they will come; thus they shall
> know that I am the Lord. (12, 16)

*   *   *

The spectacle of the humiliation of the guilty nation would
not, in spite of all, be enough to reveal the true sense of the
tragedy to other peoples. Judah's nearest neighbors showed
only indecent jubilation at the profanation of Yahveh's sanctuary
(25, 3-6). They mock at the claims that Zion had advanced for
so long, now that the proud city of David and the house of
Judah have been made to share the fate of other nations (25, 8).
Ammonites, Moabites, Edomites and Philistines cannot forget
that Jerusalem and Samaria tried to make them vassals, as David
had done, and so they greet the hour of vengeance with un-
bounded joy:

> Edom has taken vengeance on the house of Judah. (25, 12)

It can be imagined that some of them intended to gain from the situation a more material advantage than satisfaction for a payment of old scores. Edom among others would feel no repugnance to taking part in the division of the spoils, and for this they are upraided severely by Yahveh:

> Because you said: The two nations and the two lands (*Judah and Samaria*) have become mine, we shall possess them. . . .
> I will deal with you according to your anger and your envy.
> . . . I have heard all the contemptuous things you have uttered against the mountains of Israel: "They are desolate, they have been given to us to devour." (35, 10-12)

But this is precisely what Yahveh will not tolerate. No one has a right to profit by the misfortunes He inflicts on His people, because no one else, much less her ancient foes, will be allowed to triumph in her place. His hand will fall heavily on their pride and greed.

> I will inflict punishments on all their neighbors who despised them;
> thus they shall know that I, Yahveh, am their God. (28, 26)

No prophet had ever failed to follow up his threats to the chosen people with a diatribe against the foreigner. Whatever the reasons, they all concluded that Israel would not perish alone. Amos proclaimed the destruction of all the petty states round about, so that Israel might be forced to meet Yahveh face to face without any chance of escape. Because of their pride, Isaiah foretold the ruin of the nations who were the instruments of Yahveh's punishment of Israel, and also of those to whom Israel looked for help instead of bowing to the judgment of her God. Jeremiah saw, even if rather confusedly, the disappearance of the world around Israel at the same time as Israel herself.

For Ezekiel the death of the nations is necessary because it will manifest Yahveh's glory. If they were to survive the destruction of the holy city, how great would be their pride and contempt for Zion, and at the same time for the God of Zion! The old world is therefore doomed to disappear so as to avoid any lessening of God's glory.

No tree fed by water may stand by itself in its loftiness. . . .
For all of them are destined for death,
for the land below, for the company of mortals,
those who go down into the pit. (31, 14)

None of the nations rouses Ezekiel's wrath more than Tyre. The great Phoenician port had resisted the furious attacks of Babylon for thirteen years, thus proving that it was possible, if not to oppose a victorious resistance to Nebuchadnezzar, at least to hold him in check. While the army was pausing for breath, we can imagine what must have been the humiliation of the Jews at the thought that Jerusalem had not been able to hold out more than a few months, apart from the fact that Tyre's resistance was likely to arouse vain hopes in the hearts of the exiles. Worse than the attitude of Judah's other neighbors, Tyre's obstinacy was becoming for Israel "a tearing thorn" and "a brier that scratches" (28, 24). Ezekiel devotes no less than four poems to venting his anger against Tyre in a highly-colored style that brings out his poetic gifts to the best advantage. Does Tyre take herself for a god? No one is great enough to be able to oppose Yahveh's decrees:

Son of man, say to the prince of Tyre,
Because you are haughty of heart, and say,
"A god am I! I occupy a godly throne in the heart
of the sea."—And yet you are a man,
and not a god, however you may think yourself like a god.
(28, 2)

The higher the proud city has thought to rise, the more clamorous will be its fall:

> You were stamped with the seal of perfection,
> of complete wisdom and perfect beauty.
> In Eden, the garden of God you were,
> and every precious stone was your covering.
>
> With the Cherub I placed you;
> you were on the holy mountain of God,
> walking among the fiery stones.
>
> Then I banned you from the mountain of God;
> the Cherub drove you from among the fiery stones.
> You became haughty of heart because of your beauty;
> for the sake of splendor you debased your wisdom.
> I cast you to the earth, so great was your guilt;
> I made you a spectacle in the sight of kings. (28, 12-17)

The world which gazed with admiration at the valiant defense of Tyre will be a witness to her destruction and will see at the same time the destruction of their own hopes of release from Babylon's yoke.

> At the noise of your fall, at the groaning of the wounded,
> when the sword slays in your midst, shall not the isles quake?
> All the princes of the sea shall step down from their throne
> lay aside their robes, and strip off their embroidered garments.
> They shall be clothed in mourning and, sitting on the ground,
> they shall tremble at every moment and be horrified at you.
> (26, 15-16)

Ezekiel's prophecies about Tyre may not have been fulfilled immediately, but the time lag in the destruction of the city in no way invalidates the prophet's judgment that other nations will

not escape the fate of Jerusalem. All human grandeur, by its
very nature, is doomed to die.

A similar condemnation is pronounced by Ezekiel against
Egypt, the only power capable of effective resistance to the
Mesopotamian empires. The Nile kingdom, which had always
held an irresistible attraction for Palestine and the neighboring
states at critical moments in their history, still continues to
draw away God's people from their allegiance to Yahveh. Even
now, as long as there is a Pharaoh on the throne, the Israelites
will nourish the secret and fallacious hope of obtaining his
assistance, unwilling as they are to believe that their fall is final
and complete. So the prophet reminds them that Egyptian aid has
always been a snare and a delusion.

You have been a reed staff for the house of Israel.

When they leaned on you, you broke,
bringing each one of them down headlong. (29, 6-7)

To dispel the illusion, Yahveh will deliver Egypt up to
Nebuchadnezzar who will thus be compensated for his long and
vain efforts against Tyre (29, 20). Pharaoh is deceived in thinking he is safe behind the marshlands of the Nile delta:

Thus says the Lord God:
See! I am coming to you, Pharaoh, king of Egypt,
great crouching crocodile amidst your Niles;
who say, "The Niles are mine; it is I who made them!"
I will put hooks in your jaws,
and make the fish of Niles stick to your scales,
then draw you up from the midst of your Niles,
along with all the fish of your Niles sticking to your scales.
(29, 3-4)

Thus will perish what seemed to be the last chance of safety

7

for the threatened nations, and the earth will mourn, the skies will be darkened, clouds will hide the sun and the moon lose her light:

> Many peoples will be appalled at you,
> and their kings shall shudder over you in horror when
> they see me brandish my sword.
> On the day of your downfall every one of them shall
> continuously tremble for his own life. (32, 10)

*   *   *

Thus the nations will know why Yahveh has struck Israel and the fate reserved for those who like jackals lie in wait for the moment to tear the helpless corpse to pieces or push their pride to the point of thinking they can rely on their own human forces to withstand Babylon. Yahveh will mete out to all of them the same fate as his own people's.

This will be the first step in the vindication of Yahveh's glory, but by itself it would be incomplete. Destruction is not enough. Yahveh will reconstruct so that his name may everywhere be "sanctified":

> The nations shall know that I am Yahveh . . .
> when in their sight I prove my holiness through you. (36, 23)

Yahveh's glory will be still more evident in the eyes of the world when Israel is once more restored to Zion.

> My dwelling shall be with them;
> I will be their God and they shall be my people.
> Thus the nations shall know that it is I, Yahveh,
> who make Israel holy,
> when my sanctuary shall be set up among them for ever.
> (32, 27-28)

There will be an end to all doubt about the reason for Jerusalem's fall and the mystery will be cleared up.

The neighboring nations that remain shall know that I, Yahveh, have rebuilt what was destroyed, and replanted what was desolate. (36, 36)

The restoration of Israel, however, is not yet enough to heal the wound in Ezekiel's heart. Nothing, it seems, can turn him aside from his obsession; even with this, Yahveh's glory will not be restored to its fullness. The events of history are events which are confined merely to the narrow limits of time. Though they may bring compensation and restore the balance, they cannot atone for the offense to the divine name. For the reparation to be complete, all the past must be taken up again, recapitulated, condensed into a single moment in which it will be lived afresh in the glorious splendor that should have belonged to it.

Thus it is that now for the first time apocalyptic visions make their appearance in sacred literature. On the last day the whole history of the chosen people will be re-enacted. This epilogue, described by Ezekiel in two successive roughly-sketched images, shows us Yahveh fully and finally manifesting his glory to the world.

When after the restoration Israel can enjoy peace on the holy mountain, all the powers of the world will gather together against Zion to lay siege to her, and a defenseless Israel will find herself assailed by numberless hosts with Gog, king of Magog, at their head. The prophets of old had announced that Israel would be invaded from the north, but they were speaking only of Assyria and Babylon. Now it is from the remotest regions of the north, from the utmost limits of the known world, that the fearful storm will burst down upon the land with unheard-of violence, far surpassing anything that Sennacherib or Nebuchadnezzar ever dreamed of. Humanly speaking, there is not the slightest hope for the besieged city, nothing to withstand the unleashing of all the powers of evil, except absolute, uncon-ditional trust in Yahveh. Then all of a sudden the invincible power of Yahveh intervenes in full force, as when in former times he sowed panic in storm and whirlwind among the hostile armies. From the bondage in Egypt to the battles of Joshua, from the victories of the Judges to the later disasters, the whole epic story of Israel is concentrated at one point to receive its solemn ending:

> On that day, the day when Gog invades the land of Israel, my fury shall be aroused. In my anger and in my jealousy, in my fiery wrath I swear: On that day there shall be a great shaking upon the land of Israel. Before me shall tremble the fish of the sea and the birds of the air, the beasts of the field and all the reptiles that crawl upon the ground, and all men who are upon the land. Mountains shall be over-turned and cliff shall tumble, and every wall shall fall to the ground. Against him I will summon every terror. . . . I will hold judgment with him in pestilence and bloodshed, flood-ing rain and hailstones, fire and brimstone. I will rain upon his troops and upon the many peoples with him. I will prove my greatness and holiness and make myself known in the sight of many nations; thus they shall know that I am Yahveh.
>
> (38, 18-23)

The whole of the past, relived in the glory of a single, supreme event, is seen in prodigious enlargement. After dwelling on the images of universal peace already alluded to by Isaiah and the psalmists, Ezekiel's vision concludes in a Dante-like setting in a heap of weapons that will take seven years to burn away, and of corpses piled so high that it is impossible to cleanse the land from them.

In spite of the effort of imagination, Ezekiel is obviously still not satisfied with the immense picture he has painted. The splendor of Yahveh's glory will reach such a pitch that the prophet despairs of depicting it in words or images. In his impotence to proceed further he stops exhausted. He is filled with a violent and passionate longing for Yahveh's glory that was to become incorporated in the great prayer in which Jesus sums up all the aspirations that his followers should make theirs: "Hallowed be Thy name." What else did Christ wish to teach us than that he whom God has chosen involves not only his own insignificance in what he does, but also the glory of the divine name? Our sins and our failures are a crime because they injure His glory. "You seek to dishonor me" (Jn. 8, 49), Jesus was to say to the Pharisees. To atone for this injury and make reparation for the sin, nothing less could satisfy than the great sacrifice in which the drama of mankind and the mission of Christ were welded into one.

THE SECOND ISAIAH

8 Chapters 40-45 of the Book of Isaiah refer to the end of the exile. Nebuchadnezzar had died in 562. A few years later a new conqueror was to astonish the world. In 557 Cyrus became king of the Persians; in 555 he revolted against his grandfather Astyages, king of the Medes, defeated him and forced him to give up his kingdom (549). Three years later Cyrus overran Sardis and took Croesus prisoner. In 539 he invaded Babylonia, freed the captives and authorized the Jews to rebuild the temple in Jerusalem.

The name of Cyrus mentioned in the text would be enough by itself to prove that the second part of the Book of Isaiah belongs to this period. The traditional opinion, held for long, was that the prophet Isaiah had foreseen the great events that were a prelude to the restoration of Israel, but the literary unity of these fifteen chapters seems to point to the existence of a separate person who was a contemporary of the events related.

The unity of these chapters, a rarity in prophetic literature, is however broken by the insertion of four songs known as the Songs of the Servant. Though critics are not unanimous on the point, I am of the opinion that these Songs of the Servant were written by the same hand that composed the poems in the second part of the Book of Isaiah. In the absence of further knowledge this prophet is given the name of the Second or Deutero-Isaiah.

A.—EVERYTHING PASSES: ONLY THE WORD OF GOD REMAINS

After Nebuchadnezzar's victories the ancient world of the East seemed to have found a lasting equilibrium. The spoils of the Assyrian empire were shared between the Medes and the Babylonians, the two great powers left on the stage, who being in a position to counter-balance each other, for the time being at least lived in harmony. Croesus the king of Lydia, whose wealth became a legend, accepted the situation with good grace, whatever may have been his private opinion. Egypt was no longer in a position to oppose the claims of a dominant power. The stability that had been reached appeared to be likely to endure.

The calm, however, was like that which precedes a storm or an earthquake, whose approach can be suspected from the uneasiness of animals who are much closer to nature. Closer to God, the prophets likewise felt the uncertainty of the apparent peace. While Israel went its carefree way the imminence of the Assyrian menace had been foreseen by Amos. In a Babylonia apparently in a position to dominate the East for ages to come, a greater prophet whose name is unknown heard the approaching steps of a new conqueror:

Who has stirred up from the East the champion of justice, and summoned him to be his attendant? (41, 2)

Coming from beyond the mountains of Zagros, he advances swiftly and irresistibly:

To him he delivers the nations and subdues the kings; with his sword he reduces them to dust, with his bow to be driven straw. He pursues them, passing on without loss, by a path his feet do not even tread. (41, 2-3)

A prince of legendary origins, the hero of Xenophon's

Cyropedia, Cyrus set out from the distant highlands of Anshan
and supplanted his grandfather Astyages as king of the Medes.
Without delay he turned his youthful strength against Sardis
and overthrew Croesus. Soon he was at the gates of Babylon, now
no longer ruled by Nebuchadnezzar who had died in 562. The
Babylonian empire fell in 539 and its power was destroyed. Once
more the face of the world was changed and history continued
its unpredictable course.

The repercussions of Cyrus' victories were immense among
the subject peoples of Babylon, and above all among the Jews
in captivity. They all saw them as an act of vengeance, some as
the closing of a gap in their past history. But such was not the
divine plan. A world had really died, and from its ruins another
new world was about to rise.

Cyrus was a man of generous and magnanimous nature. He
respected individuals and cities, as can be seen in the case of
Lydia, where he spared Croesus and gave him an honorable
position in his service. He was not a man to deport conquered
peoples. He allowed them to remain in their own lands with
their own gods, and preferred to send them back if they had
been removed. As a Persian, the leader of a new people, he
probably realized that he had no civilization of his own to
substitute for that of the conquered or a national god to impose
on them. Whatever the case may be, he did not hesitate to
recognize the divinities and institutions of the peoples he
overcame.

The benevolent neutrality shown towards national gods,
however, began unwittingly to sap the foundations of the ancient
religious system. There could now no longer be any talk of a
god-king triumphing over his rivals in the person of the monarch,
his son and vicar. Babylon was spared, as was also her god
Marduk, but the respect paid to both had something about it
of the respect paid to the dead. The empire and the religious
economy of which they were the support were inevitably doomed
to extinction.

For the great unknown prophet all these events are not seen in the simple light of history. While from a narrowly objective viewpoint they might have seemed only a succession of happenings, the prophet discerns the profound transformation that was taking place in the world. One world, bound up with Israel's sin, was passing away forever, and the other being born was a result of the divine promise, the Word which time cannot efface.

The Second Isaiah starts from the idea that everything passes, while only the word of God remains:

All mankind is grass,
and all their glory is like the flower of the field.
The grass withers, the flower wilts,
when the breath of Yahveh blows upon it.
Though the grass withers and the flower wilts,
the word of our God stands for ever. (40, 6-8)

Thus the old Israel is dead, but Babylon which survives it is nonetheless doomed. The only reason for its existence was to provide a punishment for Israel because of her pride and hard-heartedness. Soon it will be stripped of the pride that Yahveh gave it in his wrath:

I was angry at my people, I profaned my inheritance,
and I gave them into your hand, but you showed them no
mercy....
You said, "I shall remain a sovereign mistress forever!"
(47, 6-7)

Go into darkness and sit in silence,
O daughter of the Chaldeans,
no longer shall you be called sovereign mistress of kingdoms.
(47, 5)

It will be useless for her to seek counsel in the movements

of the stars; diviners and astrologers will be consumed in the
fire like chaff. All their solemnities, like leading their idols in
triumph to the assembly of the gods and crowning their god
Marduk, acclaiming him as supreme king, will have as little
effect as they have sense. As one of these processions passes, the
prophet exclaims in mockery:

Bel bows down, Nebo stoops,
their idols are upon beasts and cattle;
they must be borne up on shoulders,
carried as burdens by the weary.
They stoop and bow down together,
unable to save those who bear them. (46, 1-2)

Nothing will save the proud city, in spite of "your many
sorceries and the great number of your spells" (47, 9) and its
cynical confidence—"You felt secure in your wickedness and you
said, 'No one sees me'" (47, 10)—or its deceptive belief in its
wisdom—"Your wisdom and your knowledge led you astray"
(47, 10). Only ruin, humiliation and death await them.

Come down, sit in the dust, O virgin daughter of Babylon;
sit on the ground, dethroned, O daughter of the Chaldeans.
(47, 1)

Babylon is passing, like all the old world which has to be
reshaped. For the old world will disappear as the grass withers
in the field. It will fall in rags like a garment eaten by moths
(51, 8). The heavens themselves "shall grow thin like smoke"
and the earth "wear out like a garment" (51, 6).

Everything passes, beginning with the world which will be
swallowed up with Israel. Everything passes, except what God
wishes to keep alive or bring back to life:

My salvation shall remain for ever,
and my justice shall never be dismayed. (51, 6)

But Israel will not die like all else that dies, nor vanish like other nations that are wiped off the face of the earth as though victims of a blind fate. In spite of the punishment which has ground them to dust, Yahveh never ceases to take care of them:

Why do you declare, O Israel,
"My way is hidden from Yahveh"? (40, 27)

Even while his people are being destroyed, Yahveh's hand does not loosen its hold. Israel remains under it even when scattered and lost in the midst of strangers and will live again after the death of the dispersion. The gift of God is given with no thought of repentance or taking back. Israel's election has been pronounced for once and all and her name is written indelibly on God's hand:

Can a mother forget her infant,
be without tenderness for the child of her womb?
Even should she forget, I will never forget you.
See, upon the palms of my hand I have written your name.
(49, 15-16)

If it has been Yahveh's will to strike the old Israel with death, he has yet decided to give it a new birth for a new destiny, in which it will be more than ever under his hand.

Fear not, I am with you;
be not dismayed, I am your God.
I will strengthen you and help you,
and uphold you with my right hand of justice ...
for I am Yahveh, your God, who grasp your right hand.
(41, 10-13)

Judah's sin has been wiped out by atonement like a cloud swept away by the wind.

I have brushed away your offenses like a cloud. (44, 22)

The bill of divorce repudiating the faithless wife has been torn up:

Speak tenderly to Jerusalem,
and proclaim to her that her service is at an end,
her guilt is expiated;
indeed, she has received from the hand of Yahveh double
for all her sins. (40, 2)

God's anger is temporary, his love is everlasting:

For a brief moment I abandoned you,
but with great tenderness I will take you back.
In an outburst of wrath, for a moment I hid my face from you;
but with enduring love I take pity on you,
says Yahveh, your redeemer. . . .
Though the mountains leave their place and the hills be shaken,
My love shall never leave you nor my covenant of peace be shaken. (54, 7-10)

        ❀   ❀   ❀

The Voice that had called Israel into existence and had been heard by Moses is once more heard by Israel in the dispersion:

Fear not, O worm Jacob, O maggot Israel,
I will help you.
Your redeemer is the Holy One of Israel. (41, 14)

There can be no mistake. Yahveh is with them. (48, 16)

This voice which threatens and comforts can speak of death or life. We are far, however, from the simple monotonous alternation on which the religious life of the ancient peoples was based. The death that it announces or confirms to Israel and to the old world of which it was a part will be complete and universal. On this point neither Jeremiah nor Ezekiel nor the Second Isaiah were mistaken. But this same voice, transcending the world and coming not from legend or popular imagination but from the infinity whence all life originates, resounds in eternity—"Heaven and earth shall pass away, but my words shall not pass away" (Matt. 24, 35)—and is the only voice that can awaken from death and summon to resurrection. This passage from death to life, of which Israel was about to have the first experience, was to become the very economy of the world's salvation:

> Unless the grain of wheat falls into the ground and dies, it remains alone. (Jn. 12, 24)

B.—YAHVEH STRETCHES HIS HAND OVER THE WHOLE WORLD

After freely choosing his people, Yahveh had always made it clear that he intended to hold them at his entire disposal. Whenever he declared his will to them, no one had been able to disobey without perishing. He was therefore the Almighty. But Israel had not learnt to understand at once the extent of his omnipotence from the definition of it given them by Yahveh himself. It came only by progressive experience. Up to now they had only been able to perceive it through their own private relations with the Godhead. Now that Yahveh comes to seek them out in Babylon, they learn for the first time that his omnipotence extends, infinite and absolute, over the whole world.

In the period around the middle of the eighth century the destiny of Israel had been closely bound up with the great events of history in the world at large, and the chosen people had had to defend their independence against Egypt and Assyria. But it had appeared clear (and the prophets had insisted on the fact) that in the clash of empires there was something more to be found than inordinate ambition, political calculation and the will to dominate. All this human pettiness was being used by God for his own ends. The initiative lay always in his hands, and it was his design that was being realized. The only reason why Sargon, Sennacherib or Nebuchadnezzar appeared on the scene was because Yahveh wished to punish his rebellious children.

Yahveh did not appear at first to be at all interested in the private affairs of other peoples when they had nothing to do with those of his own. And even when they did so, the attention he paid to other peoples appeared to be no more than what one gives to a chance agent. Everything went on as if Israel were the only people that mattered. His direct intervention in Babylon could be attributed to the fact that he wished to remain their God in whatever place they were dispersed.

It is not until we come to the eve of the Return and Restoration that the Bible begins to affirm the universality of God's power. We find Yahveh asserting his dominion over the whole world as *the sole Lord both of history and of the cosmos.* His hand holds Israel so firmly that even their death as a people cannot loosen its grasp and it will seek them out from the utmost limits of the great empire that seems to have swallowed them up:

Is my hand too short to ransom?
Have I not the strength to deliver? (50, 2)

A signal from His hand will force the nations to deliver up the children of Israel (49, 22). If they do not do so, He will come and take them from them (49, 24-25), and lead them back like a victor in battle (40, 10) or better, like a shepherd who "gathers the lambs in his arms, carrying them in his bosom" (40, 11). His power would, if necessary, gather his scattered flock from the ends of the earth:

From the east I will bring back your descendants,
from the west I will gather you.
I will say to the north: Give them up!
and to the south: Hold not back! (43, 5-6)

And that the nations shall bow down before his omnipotence,
Yahveh will also show the absolute power he wields over the
cosmos. Of this Israel has already had proof. Who was it who
struck Egypt with plagues? Who opened a path in the sea for
the Hebrews to cross? Who, to disperse the enemies of his people,
sent hornets before them, rode on the clouds of the whirlwind,
and armed Himself with hail and lightning? To bend all the
nations of the earth to his will, Yahveh is always able to do with
the universe what he pleases.

With my rebuke I dry up the sea,
I turn rivers into a desert;
their fish rot for lack of water
and die for thirst.
I clothe the heavens in mourning,
and make sackcloth their vesture. (50, 2-3)

But perhaps the nations could claim that their own gods
could do as much. It was easy for them to say so when primitive
civilizations made gods of the forces of nature and then tried to
propitiate them. Yahveh is not a cosmic deity whose power can
be sought to be appropriated. He makes use of the universe of
which he is the Creator and Lord. All is at his disposal and
nothing can dispose of him. This same Lord of the Universe who,
while earth and the heavens were shaken to their foundations,
came to meet the Hebrews not as a force of nature but as the
Almighty. It is he who will manifest himself to the whole world.
What nation would be capable of resistance to the One who
has created the firmament, fixed the stars in their courses and
called each one by name? (40, 26); the One

who has cupped in his hand the waters of the sea,
and marked off the heavens with a span,
who has held in a measure the dust of the earth,
weighed the mountains in scales and the hills in a balances?
(40, 12)

The nations are but as dust in his sight:

Behold, the nations count as a drop of the bucket,
as dust on the scales. . . .
Before him all the nations are as nought,
as nothing and void he accounts them. (40, 15-17)

Invisible, He sees all. At the time of the monarchy he watched
from his heavenly sanctuary what was happening in Palestine
and nothing of human thought and action escaped his notice.
Yet he was hidden from mortal sight by a curtain of clouds. Now
his presence is revealed as universal. His dwelling dominates
all that lives though he is still just as invisible.

He sits enthroned above the vault of the earth,
and its inhabitants are like grasshoppers;
he stretches out the heavens like a veil,
spreads them out like a tent to dwell in. (40, 22)

He is master of man's destiny, and the high and mighty on
earth are as dust before him.

He brings princes to nought,
and makes the rulers of the earth as nothing. (40, 23)

Not only does he hold every being in his glance and all life
in his hand in the present, but his power transcends time and
place, or rather envelops them. He precedes all and survives
all. He is before as he will be after.

> I, Yahveh, am the first,
> and with the last I will also be. (41, 4)

Primordial creation here acquires the sense that is now given
it by theology of an absolute beginning of creatures. God appears
as anterior to the world, and it is he who from the beginning
calls each succeeding generation to life. It should be noted,
however, that the prophet lays less stress on the idea of a creation
from nothingness than on that of anteriority. He is chiefly concerned with the Power from which nothing can escape either in
space or time, because it embraces the universe, informs and
shapes it. His glance, which has preceded all that is, sees all that
will be. His control does not follow history step by step; He
knows it all beforehand:

> in advance, things not yet done. (46, 10)
> At the beginning I foretell the outcome;

He is the true artificer, the maker of all:

> Things of the past I foretold long ago,
> they went forth from my mouth, I let you hear of them;
> then suddenly I took action and they came to be. (48, 3)

Yahveh's power over the world is therefore absolute:

> I am God, yes, from eternity I am He;
> there is none who can deliver from my hand;
> who can countermand what I do? (43, 13-14)

Such is the power that promises to bring back Israel to life
after the dispersion. And as such it shows itself also in the
phenomenon of Cyrus. The conqueror whose blitzkriegs and
astounding victories are filling the East with his youthful glory

has been raised up by Yahveh. Behind him, where all will turn
their gaze, is the unseen but operative presence of God:

> My friend shall do my will against Babylon and the progeny
> of Chaldea;
> I myself have spoken, I have called him,
> I have brought him and his way succeeds. (48, 14-15)

All history, in fact, is gravitating around the reconstruction
of the holy city and its temple:

> I say of Cyrus: My shepherd, who fulfills my every wish;
> he shall say of Jerusalem, "Let her be rebuilt,"
> and of the temple, "Let its foundations be laid." (44, 28)

And the return of Israel:

> He shall let my exiles go free without price or ransom.
> (45, 13)

❋   ❋   ❋

Yahveh's supreme dominion was therefore only discovered by
Israel in the light of actual events. But the sudden discovery
did not face them with a formidable master to be adored in fear
and trembling, but with a loving and patient Father bending
his power to draw his children from the nothingness into which
he had plunged them:

> I am Yahveh, your God, who grasp your right hand;
> it is I who say to you, "Fear not, I will help you." (41, 13)

It is difficult here not to make a comparison between the
realistic procedure of biblical revelation and the abstract,
dogmatic conception of the Koran. Mahomet wished to confront

man directly with the majesty of the one and only God by affirming the omnipotence of Allah from the height of his own
authority. From the beginning the Bible leads Israel gradually
to understand that Yahveh's hand is laid on them. It is only
later, after more than half a millennium through events that
testify to the paternal intervention of Yahveh in the troublous
life of his people, that Israel comes to a knowledge of the universal, almighty power of her God as a truth learned from experience. Where the Koran only succeeds in crushing the believer
under an inhuman transcendence of God, the Bible reaches the
same conclusion from history as lived by the chosen people. The
God of the Bible himself reveals his transcendence, by events as
they occur and through these same events, for his way of in-
structing his children and showing them the mystery of himself·
is to make use of everything that offers itself. "For those who
love God all things work together unto good" (Rom. 8, 28).

C.—FROM THE CREATION TO THE COMING OF THE KINGDOM OF YAHVEH

How beautiful upon the mountains
are the feet of him who brings glad tidings,
announcing peace, bearing good news,
announcing salvation,
and saying to Zion,
"Your God is King!"

Hark! Your watchmen raise a cry,
together they shout for joy,
for they see directly, before their eyes,
Yahveh restoring Zion. (52, 7-8)

The Voice sounding in a doomed world announces to the
exiles not only that they will be brought back from among the
nations, but that by God's almighty power Israel will have its
place on the map from which it had been blotted out. The God
who exists before everything that is, in whom events and creatures

have their origin and who foresees all, is about to gather up the scattered remnants of his people and establish a new kingship with them in the land they will again occupy. This restoration accomplished by the God of Israel's free initiative can be compared only to the act of creation which produced the world from chaos.

All sedentary peoples, it is true, hoped in the coming of an age of peace and prosperity during which their god would reign, but they saw it as a return to the primal harmony of creation. To recover its original purity, vitiated to the very sources of life by the sin of men, the cosmos would, they thought, have to undergo periodic regeneration.

In Babylon, for instance, the prince would take upon himself the sins of the whole nation and every year be stripped of his power, humiliated and held up to scorn. A general state of license was intended to represent the return of the earth to primitive chaos, and disorder prevailed until the national god had been again proclaimed king in the assembly of the gods. Then, as in the time of his victory over the sea monsters, he would reassume his rule over the world and once more invest the monarch, his son, by calling him by his name and taking him by the right hand. The country would then recover its former vigor.

The Bible had broken with this cyclic idea. Salvation was not to be found in a perpetual return to a starting point, but in an unceasing progression towards a goal known only to God. Thus Israel announced the ordeal of purification which would assure the final triumph of Yahveh, his eternal kingship and the unfailing happiness of the new people. The course of history begun on Mount Sinai would have an end in the holy mountain.

The Second Isaiah takes up an idea only barely hinted at by Jeremiah and, over and beyond Sinai, refers the process back to Creation itself. The reason he develops this theme so strongly is that he stresses the identity of the God of Creation with the God who is Israel's leader. The God who created the world is the same God who will bring his people back to life and establish them in the final peace of the New Covenant. Creation is therefore more the starting point of a great and irreversible evolution than the archetype to which successive generations should conform.

The idea of creation had hardly entered the minds of the prophets before him. They could not see how it fitted in with the drama of the covenant which was their main concern. But the relationship was made evident and necessary by the New Covenant. The creation of a new Israel supposed the initiative of a God who was supreme over life and death whether his own people or the world itself was in question. There could be no difference between this initiative on his part and that which was present at Creation. This is stressed by the prophet in a passage in which he recalls the old pagan myth of the combat in which the god overcame the power of the sea monsters, transferring it to the might of Yahveh's arm:

> Awake, awake, put on strength,
> O arm of Yahveh!
> Awake as in the days of old,
> in ages long ago!
> Was it not you who crushed Rahab,
> you who pierced the Dragon?
> Was it not you who dried up the sea,
> the waters of the great deep? (51, 9-10)

      ❀   ❀   ❀

Could the free act of creation, after all, remain an isolated act? Could the power which had brought the cosmos into being be shown only on this one single occasion? Quite the contrary, this initiative on the part of a creative God called for a whole succession of initiatives just as free and voluntary. The demiurge is the same all-seeing God who keeps watch over all things and whose hand is always over Israel.

Like a prelude announcing the essential motifs of a symphony, Creation contains in embryo all the modes of God's action throughout history. Such, for example, is the will for order and light which is declared in Genesis and expressed again in the work of restoration:

Thus says Yahveh, the creator of the heavens,
who is God, the designer and maker of the earth,
who established it, not creating it to be a waste,
but designing it to be lived in.
"I am Yahveh, and there is no other.
I have not spoken from hiding,
nor from some dark place of the earth,
and I have not said to the descendants of Jacob,
'Look for me in an empty waste.'" (45, 18-19)

In the creation of the world Israel is able more clearly to see features which recall the beginnings of her own history. With or without reference to an original combat, it is represented as the victorious action of Yahveh against the tumultuous power of the waves in establishing the earth above the waters. In like manner by dividing the sea with his arm Yahveh opens up a passage for his people to escape from the pursuit of Pharaoh. Thus at the end of a verse in passage quoted above, in which Yahveh's victory over Rahab and the Dragon is celebrated, a gloss has been added on purpose:

... who made the depths of the sea into a way for the redeemed to pass over. (51, 10)

The Exodus was therefore one of the free acts of God in which the work of creation was prolonged and shown more clearly, but it was only a foreshadowing of the return of the exiles. In both cases a people, then not important and now no longer

so, is assembled to traverse deserts under the sole guidance of
God, and from him they receive life:

> Thus says Yahveh,
> who opens a way in the sea,
> and a path in the mighty waters. . . .
> Remember not the events of the past,
> the things of long ago consider not.
> See, I am doing something new!
> Now it springs forth, do you not perceive it?
> In the desert I made a way,
> in the wasteland, rivers. (43, 16-19)

Thus there is the same initiative on the part of Yahveh, the
same solicitude for his people on the march through vast and
desolate country, the same demand for absolute trust in his
guidance:

> They did not thirst when he led them through dry lands;
> water from the rocks he set flowing for them. (48, 21)

> Along the ways they shall find pastures,
> on every bare height shall their pastures be.
> They shall not hunger or thirst,
> nor shall the scorching wind or the sun strike them,
> for he who pities them leads them
> and guides them beside springs of water.
> I will cut a road through all my mountains,
> and make my highways level. (49, 9-11)

As when his cloud escorted the Hebrews in the desert, now
in front and now behind them, Yahveh will envelop his people
with His presence.

> Yahveh comes before you,
> and your rear guard is the God of Israel. (52, 12)

Creation, Exodus, return from exile are three decisive moments chosen by Yahveh to draw out existence from nothingness and create life as symbolized by the living water:

I will open up rivers on the bare heights,
and fountains in the broad valleys;
I will turn the desert into a marshland,
and the dry ground into springs of water. (41, 18)

To produce the joy of light from darkness:

I will lead the blind on their journey. . . .
I will turn darkness into light before them. (42, 16)

＊　　＊　　＊

From creation the cosmos had arisen, and from the Exodus the people of God. From the Return, the third stage in the work of creation, would be born the new Israel, the people of the New Covenant.

To describe its coming the prophet has recourse to the terminology used from ancient times in the East for the investiture of a king. Like a king, the sovereign people has been chosen:

You, Israel, my servant Jacob, whom I have chosen,
offspring of Abraham my friend! (41, 8; cf. 4, 1)

Yahveh has called them by name, and the significance of being called by name is evident:

I have called you by name; you are mine. (43, 1; cf. 45, 3)

Yahveh has grasped them by the right hand (41, 13) after having formed them from the womb (44, 2, 21, 24; 43, 1).

These are not empty formulas. Israel is from henceforth really a king. The royal line of David has been replaced by the whole nation which thereby inherits the promises made to the king:

> I will renew with you the everlasting covenant,
> the benefits assured to David. (55, 3)

The ancient formulas now acquire a new and striking significance. No monarch invested by a god-king could ever, as Israel does Yahveh, hail him as his Creator and his King. Yahveh has for the third time given life to Israel, but it must be repeated that there is no comparison between this third "moment" of creation and the early renewal that followed the symbolic degradation of the Babylonian king at the feast of Akitu. The chosen people must not forget that from the very beginning their life had been nothing but sin:

> Your first father sinned,
> your spokesmen rebelled against me.
> Your princes profaned my holy place.
> Therefore I put Jacob under the ban,
> and exposed Israel to scorn. (43, 27-28)

Their sin had been borne by Yahveh with unfailing patience. Nothing in the attitude of Israel could persuade Him to go back on the inevitable judgment:

> Yet you did not call upon me, O Jacob,
> for you grew weary of me, O Israel.
> You did not bring me sheep for your holocausts,
> nor honor me with your sacrifices . . .
> instead, you burdened me with your sins,
> and wearied me with your crimes.
> It is I, I, who wipe out, for my own sake, your offenses;
> your sins I remember no more. (43, 22-25)

The religious adventure of Israel must begin again from the starting point by a free act of God's liberality. Like Abraham, the "friend" of God (41, 8), in order to be born again the servant of Yahveh must expect nothing but the promise and the blessing of the Most High. The attitude of this patriarch must be a model for that of the new Israel:

Look to the rock from which you were hewn,
the pit from which you were quarried;
look to Abraham your father,
and to Sarah who gave you birth;
when he was but one I called him,
I blessed him and made him many. (51, 1-2)

After recreating a people fo himself, Yahveh will remake a country in which he will reign, for Jerusalem is destroyed. She lies dead drunk after drinking of the cup of God's wrath:

Awake, awake!
Arise, O Jerusalem,
you who drank at Yahveh's hand the cup of His wrath;
who drained to the dregs the bowl of staggering! (51, 17)

But now she is called back to life by the all-powerful word:

Shake off the dust,
ascend to the throne, Jerusalem;
loose the bonds from your neck,
O captive daughter of Zion! (52, 2)

The voice that dried up oceans to let the land emerge is now heard calling the dead cities back to life:

I say to Jerusalem: Be inhabited;
to the cities of Judah: Be rebuilt. (44, 26)

At His command
your rebuilders make haste,
those who tore you down and laid you waste
go forth from you. (49, 17)

Zion, chief city of the nations, will soon be able from the
the top of her mountain to acclaim the arrival of Yahveh bringing his children in his arms:

Go up onto a high mountain, Zion,
herald of glad tidings![1]
... Here comes with power the Lord Yahveh,
who rules by his strong arm ....
Like a shepherd he feeds his flock;
in his arms he gathers the lambs. (40, 9-11)

The city will be too small to contain all the people of God:

Look about and see,
they are all gathering and coming to you. ...
The children whom you had lost shall yet say to you,
"This place is too small for me,
make room for me to live in."
You shall ask yourself, "Who has borne me these?
I was bereft and barren; who has reared them?" (49, 18, 20-21)

Who else but the God who opened the barren wombs of the
wives of the patriarchs will thus multiply the children of the
forsaken city?

---

1. To make a personified Jerusalem the messenger of Yahveh's return to the
other cities of Judah may at first sight appear strange. It must be remembered, however, that in the ancient liturgies of divine monarchy the
capital city and its temple had a particular significance quite distinct from
other cities of the country. This is borne out by the fact that in the Hebrew
text "herald" is feminine, in apposition to "Zion."

Raise a glad cry, you barren one who did not bear,
break forth in jubilant song, you who were not in labor,
for more numerous are the children of the deserted wife
than the children of her who has a husband. (54, 1)

The nations awaited from their god-king the renewal of a
latent life, but at the voice of Yahveh Israel arises from death. As
lifegiving water might spring from the barren desert, so from
barrenness springs a numerous progeny:

I will pour out water upon the thirsty ground,
and streams upon the dry land;
I will pour out my spirit upon your offspring,
and my blessing upon your descendants.
They shall spring up amid the verdure
like poplars beside the flowing waters. (44, 3-4)

When Yahveh has finally remade his country and his people
he will inaugurate his reign. And then there will be final, total
peace, the peace dreamed of by the prophets of former times.
Founded on justice, the holy city will be under Yahveh's protection and will remain forever, invulnerable:

In justice shall you be established,
far from the fear of oppression,
where destruction cannot come near you.
Should there be any attack, it shall not be of my making;
whoever attacks you shall fall before you.
Lo, I have created the craftsman who blows on the burning
coals
and forges weapons as his work;
It is I also who have created the destroyer to work havoc;
no weapon fashioned against you shall prevail. (54, 14-17)

The dream of universal harmony, a dream that had always

haunted the imagination of mankind, the unknown prophet proclaims will come true not just by looking back to consider the lessons of history, but by advancing deliberately towards a future in which God will intervene once more to bring to a conclusion the marvelous design of which Creation was the first act.

In so far as it is the work of God, this design continues without pause whatever man may do, and whatever his fundamental unwillingness to cooperate. But God makes use of the events that are a consequence of man's actions to remodel the rebellious clay with his all-powerful hand. There is therefore throughout the ages a marvelous sequence of creation ever improving on the old and bringing out its details more clearly. When one model seems to have been destroyed and the clay returned to a shapeless mass, another finer model arises from it. A primitive man dies to his native land and becomes Abraham, an uncertain wanderer guided only by God who has called him. His posterity dies to the fertile land of Goshen where they are in bondage, in order to traverse an interminable desert in which God makes of them not only a people but his own special people. This people, abusing God's gift of the promised land, dies under the mortal blows of ambitious empires so as to learn anew the obedience God wishes from it, and from its death a new people arises, still imperfect but at least knowing that God must be served from the innermost heart without coming to terms with the rest of the world still buried in darkness. And this new Israel, on whose shoulders the garment of sin was still to lie, would die with the divine Mediator, to be born again fully conscious at last of the demands of its untiring Creator.

The clay does not take shape of itself but by the will of the divine Modeller who time after time seems to be destroying his work, only to refashion it again in a more perfect manner. Nothing more is asked of the clay than that it should allow itself to be molded, destroyed and remodelled. Once the perfect figure has left the Creator's hands, is not this the destiny which is reserved for each one of us who are copies of the divine Exemplar? He holds us in his hands and with innumerable temporary deaths draws out our life, which is his life and which he wishes to give us in its fullness.

D.—UNIVERSAL SIGNIFICANCE OF THE RESTORATION OF ISRAEL

Yahveh was about to seek out his dispersed people and, gathering them together again, would show himself to be undisputed Lord of the cosmos and of history. The founding of his kingdom in Jerusalem would be a new act of his omnipotence, and Israel would occupy an even more privileged position in the world, the very center of the universe it might be said. Was all this to happen so that Israel might selfishly enjoy the benefits her God bestowed upon her, or did it mean rather that with regard to the world she was to assume a responsibility proportionate to the favors received?

         ❋   ❋   ❋

As has been seen, Israel had quite early had the impression that her destiny, one so much out of the ordinary, was of such a nature as to interest other peoples as well. It was for this reason she had always shown herself very sensitive as to how others might judge her. But, more than national pride, it was especially Yahveh's glory that was at stake.

Ezekiel had been tormented by the idea of restoring the divine name in all its glory. The Second Isaiah is less obsessed with this, for with the passing of time the humiliation of the exile and the fall of the holy city had evidently lost some of its sting. The sanctification of Yahveh's name, however, does not leave him indifferent. He is aware that if Yahveh has intervened so constantly in Israel's favor, it is for the sake—and only for the sake—of his name:

For the sake of my name I restrain my anger,
for the sake of my renown I hold it back from you,

lest I should destroy you. . . .
For my sake, for my own sake, I do this;
why should I suffer profanation?
My glory I will not give to another. (48, 9-11)

Hence, since Yahveh's glory is so closely involved, the return
from exile cannot take place on the quiet. An event so pregnant
with meaning will be witnessed clearly by the whole world:

Yahveh has bared his holy arm
in the sight of all the nations;
all the ends of the earth shall behold
the salvation of our God. (52, 10)

To describe the joy of these days of triumph the Second Isaiah
uses, in reverse, the same procedure as his predecessors had done
to make the threats in their message strike the imagination of
their hearers. They would follow up what they had to say with
lamentations in a liturgical style, as if the threatened misfortune
had already arrived and the people were engaged in mourning
rites because of it. It is the procedure of narrating in the present
without reference to chronology, so that past and future are seen
in the present by the listener.

Thus the pages of the Second Isaiah are filled with the songs
of joy he hears beforehand. The announced return is already being
celebrated with thanksgivings in the form of ritual hymns breaking into the prophetic message. This is easily understandable
when one thinks what a glorious ending there was to be to Israel's
tragic fate. Such an ending could hardly be hailed otherwise
than with a hymn of exultation in which joy for liberation and a
renewal of life are the prominent themes. But there is also another
theme, more deeply felt even than this joy—the adoring confession
that it is the will of God and another witness to the glory of the
divine name:

You shall rejoice in Yahveh,
and glory in the Holy One of Israel. (41, 16)

Since everything has been begun by God, everything that
follows must be attributed to God:

The people whom I formed for myself
shall announce my praise. (43, 21)

An act of thanksgiving is not something that can be kept secret.
When the prayer of a poor man had been heard, he would in-
vite all his friends to go with him to offer a sacrifice of praise (the
tôda), thus giving public witness to what Yahveh had deigned
to do for him. In the same way Israel will shout aloud her joy
before the world:

With shouts of joy proclaim this, make it known;
publish it to the ends of the earth,
and say, "Yahveh has redeemed his servant Jacob." (48, 20)

Nature joins in the joy of the redeemed people and their song
of praise. She renews and adorns herself to welcome those returning home:

Yes, in joy you shall depart,
in peace shall you be brought back;
mountains and hills shall break out in song before you,
and all the trees of the countryside shall clap their hands.
In the place of the thornbush the cypress shall grow,
instead of nettles, the myrtle. (55, 12-13)

The earth which had broken the bonds of fellowship with the
guilty people delights to receive back the exiles on whom God
has had compassion (49, 13); it acclaims the manifestation of
Yahveh's glory (44, 23) and places the final seal on the work

of creation. It is in fact a "new song" that all creation will intone, from sea to mountain and from city to desert:

> Sing to Yahveh a new song,
> his praise from the ends of the earth:
> let the sea and what fills it resound,
> the coastlands, and those who dwell in them.
> Let the steppe and its cities cry out,
> the villages where Kedar dwells;
> let the inhabitants of Sela exult,
> and shout from the top of the mountains.
> Let them give glory to Yahveh,
> and utter his praise in the coastlands. (42, 10-12)

We can already hear the voice of St. Paul:

> The eager longing of creation awaits the revelation of the sons of God. (Rom. 8, 19)

Nor shall the nations be excluded from this triumphal spectacle. To them, too, Yahveh's glory will be shown in all its splendor:

> All mankind shall know that I, Yahveh, am your savior,
> Your redeemer, the Mighty One of Jacob. (49, 26)

Then they cannot but join in the universal chorus of praise.

✿   ✿   ✿

Though the Second Isaiah may insist less than Ezekiel on the need to reestablish the glory of the divine name in all its fullness, he is more than ever profoundly convinced of the universal character of the national restoration.

Jeremiah before him had touched lightly on the idea that

the salvation of Israel was a prelude to the world's, but he gives no indication of what advantage the other nations (with the exception of Moab) will draw from the renewal of the Covenant. That the experience of Israel is meant to be a lesson for the world rather than a mere spectacle is the thought that becomes prominent with the Second Isaiah. The restoration of the chosen people will herald universal redemption.

It is in the nature of a lesson that to serve its purpose it must be heard, and must destroy ignorance and error before it can inculcate truth. In contrast to Israel's joy for her new-found salvation, and nature's joy not only at witnessing it but in finding a further harmony in it, the nations will begin by recognizing to their shame that hitherto they have been attached to fictitious gods who were incapable of saving them:

> They shall be turned back in utter shame
> who trust in idols;
> who say to molten images,
> "You are our gods." (42, 17; cf. 45, 20)

These imaginary gods had to be carried on beasts of burden at the festivals of Akitu, but it is Yahveh himself who carries his people (46, 1-4).

Some of them will have to walk chained through the streets of Jerusalem in order to make the evidence all the clearer to them. Then they will be obliged to confess to those who have vanquished them:

> "With you only is God, and nowhere else;
> the gods are nought."
> Truly with you God is hidden,
> the God of Israel, the savior! (45, 14-15)

In short, all will know with certainty that their gods were of no avail, and the only living God is he who has been able to bring a dead people back to life. But to acknowledge this God whose prodigies cannot be denied implies a sharing in the monotheistic belief of the Jewish people. Confession of this belief will be required of all.

It may be said in passing that the monotheistic belief of the Jews was not the result of philosophical speculation but of an experience. Though the nations had not had the direct benefit of this experience as had Israel, yet they could still be instructed by meditating on Israel's experience:

> You are my witnesses!
> Is there a God or any Rock besides me? (44, 8)

If they wish to defend their impotent gods, let them show, if they can, what benefits they have received from them:

> Let all the nations gather together,
> let the peoples assemble! ...
> Let them produce witnesses to prove themselves right,
> that one may hear and say, "It is true!" (43, 9)

Let them compare their own illusions with all that Yahveh has done for Israel as so many proofs of his power and goodness. Or rather, to help them, let Israel raise her voice in witness:

> You are my witnesses, says Yahveh,
> my servants whom I have chosen to know and believe in me
> and understand that it is I. . . .
> It is I, I Yahveh;
> there is no savior but me.
> It is I who foretold, I who saved and made it known. . . .
> You are my witnesses says Yahveh,
> I am God,
> Yes, from eternity I am He;
> there is none who can deliver from my hand. (43, 10-12)

The lesson, after humiliating, will be a source of comfort.
Since Yahveh is not only the one God, but also the only possible
savior, the nations in their turn can hope in him.

Turn to me and be safe,
all you ends of the earth,
for I am God;
there is no other! (45, 22)

In the process of instruction Israel will have a vital part to
play, and it will not be merely that of a simple witness:

Behold, I have given you as a witness for the peoples,
a leader and a commander of nations. (55, 4)

        ❖ ❖ ❖

How will Israel become a teacher of the nations and enable
them to profit from her own salvation?
The prophet sees the kings prostrate on their knees before
the victorious people:

Bowing to the ground they shall worship you and lick the dust
at your feet (49, 23; cf. 45, 24-25)

and fellaheen of the Nile, merchants of Kush and tall Sabeans
marching in chains through the new Jerusalem (45, 14). But this
submission is an imperfect one, as it is only exterior. The unknown prophet seems to have conceived the domination of Israel
in a much more profound sense if, as seems probable, the Songs
of the Servant are to be attributed to him.
Without going into questions of exegesis, it will be enough to
state the conclusions arrived at after an attentive examination of
the evidence available. The Servant of Yahveh appears to represent first and foremost the people of the New Covenant, and in

the second place a central personage in whom the new people finds its most perfect expression and sees its spiritual experience fully realized. The Servant would seem to signify, therefore, both the new Israel as a whole, as well as the personage who epitomizes her, the ideal prophet of whom Jeremiah seems to have been the type.

This future prophet, like Jeremiah himself, will have a mission not only to establish the new people around the new experience he is to live through, but also to teach the nations:

> It is too little for you to be my servant,
> to raise up the tribes of Jacob,
> and restore the survivors of Israel;
> I will make you a light to the nations,
> that my salvation may reach to the ends of the earth.
>
> (49, 6; cf. 42, 6)

What the prophet will have to communicate to all nations is a commandment, a law which will assure their salvation:

> A bruised reed he shall not break,
> and a smoldering wick he shall not quench,
> until he establishes justice on the earth;
> and the coastlands will wait for his teaching. (42, 3-4)

From experience Israel knows that the worship of idols leads to death, and that faith in Yahveh is the only means of finding the way to life:

> Though I thought I had toiled in vain, and for nothing,
> uselessly, spent my strength,
> yet my reward is with Yahveh,
> my recompense is with my God. (49, 4)

No one better than Israel could therefore let the nations under-

stand that the sin for which she stood condemned was exactly
the same as theirs, in which they had had the weakness to share.
Such would seem to be the sense of the famous messianic verses:

Yet it was our infirmities that he bore,
our sufferings that he endured . . .
he was pierced for our offenses,
crushed for our sins. (53, 4-5[1])

According to this interpretation, by these words the nations
will acknowledge that if Israel has been punished it is because
she allowed herself to follow their example. They will therefore
have no cause to accuse the chosen people:

We thought of him as stricken,
as one stricken by God and afflicted. (53, 4)

In Israel's condemnation it is their own that they are bound
to hear.

Yahveh laid upon him the guilt of us all. . . .
We had all gone astray like sheep,
each following his own way. (53, 6)

But at the same time Israel shows them the remedy which,
after saving her, can save all of them in the same way:

Upon him was the chastisement that makes us whole,
by his stripes we were healed. (53, 5)

Whatever may be the exact meaning of this whole passage,

1. This is the interpretation given to these verses by Henri Cazelles "Les
Poèmes du Serviteur, leur place, leur structure, leur théologie" (**Recherches
de Science Religieuse,** January-March 1955).

the *Songs of the Servant* are a sure testimony that the faith shown by Israel in the midst of adversity is offered to the whole world as the sole means of salvation. At the triumph of the one whom they had loaded with contempt, the kings themselves will be seized with fear.

> Thus says Yahveh, the redeemer and the Holy One of Israel,
> to the one despised, whom the nations abhor,
> the slave of rulers:
> "When kings see you they shall stand up,
> and princes shall prostrate themselves because of Yahveh who
> is faithful." (49, 7)

The greatness of the event, with its origin in the deepest human misery and abjection and owing nothing to what men take pride in, stands as a challenge to the powerful ones of the world. It shows them a new order of things transcending worldly values and turning its ordinary economy upside down:

> They shall see what they have not been told,
> and understand what they have not heard. (52, 15)

The "mystery" which is thus displayed to them confounds the great ones of the earth and they stand speechless (52, 15), no doubt with astonishment, but also perhaps with their hands pressed to their lips in sign of adoration, for it is the divine glory which is manifested in the "glorified" (55, 5) and "exalted" (52, 13) Servant. He appears, in fact, to be raised to the same level as God, as if the prophet already foresaw the triumph of the Son of Man, whose epiphany was yet to be described in the Book of Daniel.

The law bringing freedom which Israel is to proclaim and spread among the nations is essentially a law of humility and faith. By bearing witness to her own experience she will be their ruler. She will not impose herself on them by force, but by the example of her complete trust in God.

> Upon him I have put my spirit;
> he shall bring forth judgment to the nations,
> not crying out, not shouting,
> not making his voice heard in the street . . .
> in trust he shall bring forth judgment. (42, 1-4)

✿ ✿ ✿

It was to be in the same way that Christ would establish his kingship over the world, gathering mankind around the Cross, the tomb, and the hilltop of the Ascension:

> And I, if I be lifted up from the earth, will draw all things to myself. (Jn. 12, 32)

The Jews never had dreams of conquest. They had known only bondage in Egypt and destitution in the wilderness when Yahveh gave them the gift of the Promised Land, and by their repeated sins they let it escape from their hands. Then when Yahveh brought them back to it, they waited there in the faith that the peoples would come thronging to Jerusalem. For it was not for God's chosen one to go down towards the nations, but for them to come up. This is another point on which the Bible and the Koran are poles apart. When the Moslems broke out of their own land, they did so to plunder in the name of Allah; any possibility of world expansion was denied them once they found themselves confined to the territories they had conquered. The Old Testament, on the other hand, by presenting the experience of Israel as a lesson for all mankind opened up a wide and splendid path for Christian universalism.

E.—FORMATION PERIOD OF THE NEW COVENANT

In order that the restoration announced by the prophet might truly crown the work of creation, that the nations might with profit receive the teaching which would subdue them to the commandment (the "judgment") of the living God, and that it should be shown from actual experience that the lowest and most despised of peoples could, by God's power, be drawn out of their obscurity to fulfill a glorious destiny, it was necessary that Yahveh should find the new Israel an instrument perfectly docile to his will. Israel could not teach the world justice unless she were first just herself:

The just one, my Servant, shall give justice to many,
and their guilt he shall bear. (53, 11)

The final triumph requires unshakeable faith and total surrender on the part of Yahveh's Servant. However overwhelmed he may be, he will be clothed with the strength of God if he allows it to act within him.

It is a tired man that the word of God awakens in the morning. It awakens my ear in the morning that I may hear as they that are taught. (50, 4)

For, if the disciple is attentive, it is in order to obey his Master unreservedly:

My Lord Yahveh has opened my ear,
and I have not rebelled, have not turned back. (50, 5)

He will accept the ordeal of punishment with trusting sumission:

Yahveh was pleased to crush him in infirmity. (53, 10)

Even more, he will offer himself of his own accord to suffering as a sacrifice of reparation:

If he gives himself as an offering for sin . . .
the will of Yahveh shall be accomplished through him.
(53, 10)

The sacrifice will be accomplished by him steadfastly and uncomplainingly:

I gave my back to those who beat me,
my cheeks to those who plucked my beard.
My face I did not shield from buffets and spitting. (50, 6)

Because of this, Yahveh will be his support, his strength and his safety in the very midst of his trials:

My Lord Yahveh is my help,
therefore I am not disgraced;
I have set my face like flint,
knowing that I shall not be put to shame. (50, 7)

The judgments of men cannot affect him, for they only serve to bring out the justice of God:

If anyone wishes to oppose me, let us appear together!
Who disputes my right? Let him confront me!
See, my Lord Yahveh is my help;
who will prove me wrong? (50, 8-9)

Hence he will not lower himself to justify himself before his persecutors:

Like a lamb led to the slaughter
or a sheep before the shearers,
he was silent and opened not his mouth. (53, 7)

Such is the portrait the Second Isaiah draws of the Servant who is to accomplish God's design. Without a care for the world's judgments he entrusts himself completely to God's hands; he effaces himself before the infinite Will; he empties himself so that the Almighty may take full possession of him. We can already hear the words of St. Paul:

My grace is enough for you;
my strength finds its full scope in your weakness.

(2 Cor. 12, 9)

Never before had the spiritual terms of the Covenant been so strongly affirmed. But were the exiles ready to implement these terms? Yahveh bids them do so, as though their hearts were henceforth open to his law and their wills subject to his:

Hear me, you who know justice,
you people who have my teaching at heart. (51, 7)

Yet he is obliged to recognize that his appeal evokes no response:

Why was no one there when I came?
Why did no one answer when I called? (50, 2)

Where is the disciple with open ears?

Lead out the people who are blind though they have eyes,
who are deaf though they have ears. (43, 8)

Who is blind but my servant,
or deaf like the messenger I send? (42, 19)

Where he expected to find intrepid faith the prophet finds only pusillanimity:

Listen to me you faint-hearted,
you who seem far from the victory of justice. (46, 12)

Yahveh needs to be endlessly comforting his children who are
ever ready to feel discouraged:

Fear not, I am with you;
be not dismayed, I am your God. (41, 10)

Fear not, O worm Jacob, O maggot Israel. (41, 14; cf. 43, 1-5)

It is difficult to recognize the new Israel in this people which
needs, just as before, to be urged to conversion:

Remember this and be ashamed,
bear it well in mind, you rebels! (46, 8)

It looks still like the old Israel, deaf to all admonition:

You are stubborn,
your neck is an iron sinew,
your forehead bronze. . . .
Now that you have heard, look at all this;
must you not admit it? (48, 4-6)

We seem to hear the voices of former prophets reproaching
Israel with her rebellion against God from the beginning:

Hear this, O house of Jacob,
called by the name Israel,
sprung from the stock of Judah,
you who swear by the name of Yahveh
and invoke the God of Israel
without sincerity or justice. (48, 1)

Where is the new Israel? Into what hands has the great design been entrusted?

* * *

And yet the great design was to be accomplished with time, as the acorn does not become an oak tree in a day. The prophets saw things in a different perspective from that of history. Succeeding stages become confused in the eyes of these visionaries, and distant ones often appear as close at hand. Moreover it is evident that it is much simpler and takes far less time to assemble a band of captive herdsmen and peasants and lead them into a new land than to move individual wills, win over hearts and inspire devotion to a cause. To establish the Old Covenant it was enough for Yahveh to raise up Moses and guide him through the desert. But the New Covenant had to reckon with human freedom which by its nature gives consent only upon understanding. Jeremiah may well have preached an interior and personal religion, but to establish itself on the ruins of a thousand-year-old tradition of collective worship it needed the work and effort of many generations. The effort alone could not have produced results without a living example to support it. An integral and perfect experience was needed to sustain and clarify the individual experience that would be required from each member of the community. It was necessary that one man should satisfy all the requirements of the New Covenant so that each one's spiritual conduct could be conformed to that of this exemplar.

His role, foreshadowed in Jeremiah and in part taken by him, is attributed by the Second Isaiah to the Servant of Yahveh who now acquires the personal features of an individual who is the embodiment of the whole nation. The Servant must, above all, accept of his own accord the ordeal of death (53, 8-9) which will gain salvation and an enduring posterity for Israel:

If he gives his life as an offering for sin,
he shall see his descendants in a long life. (53, 10)

The idea of a death would atone for the sins of a whole people
was not unknown in the ancient world. At the festival of Akitu,
as we have seen, the monarch pretended to die as a form of expiation, but his death was only a symbolic one, automatically
followed by re-investiture. But the case is quite different with
the Servant of Yahveh. He too, it is true, intercedes for sinners:

He shall take away the sins of many,
and win pardon for their offenses. (53, 12)

He does not do so, however, by virtue of his royal dignity but
by the fullness of his spiritual experience and the perfection of
his faith. He does not present himself as a prince responsible
for his people before the divinity, but by his sacrifice he becomes
the promoter of a new economy of salvation, valid for all who
accept to follow in his footsteps:

I formed you and set you as a covenant of the people,
a light for the nations. (42, 6)

As Mediator of the Covenant, the Servant of Yahveh is a
successor, not of the Davidic kings who never had such a function, but of Moses and the prophets, of whom Jeremiah was the
most accomplished example until he himself, the Prophet *par excellence,* brought to the prophetic office an incomparable rich-
ness and splendor.

For the moment, however, the appearance of the Servant and
of the new Israel which he alone will be capable of raising up is
hidden in the distant future, but at least the ideal is present.
The New Covenant exists in the state of hope now that the
promise has been solemnly ratified by Yahveh. Such a promise is

equal to a certitude; it was reliance on the same promise that led Abraham to leave Chaldea, and Moses to guide his people through the desert. From now on the Israelites are called to become part of a regenerate world which is still only virtually in existence:

Seek Yahveh while he may be found,
call him while he is near.
Let the scoundrel forsake his way,
and the wicked man his thoughts.
Let him turn to the Yahveh for mercy,
to our God who is generous in forgiving. (55, 6-7)

Israel the harlot is buried for ever in the winding sheet of the past. The former sinful people has disappeared with the fall of Jerusalem. Already we can catch a glimpse of the features of the faithful spouse, Wisdom, whom we shall see inviting her disciples to the banquet she has herself prepared:

All you who are thirsty, come to the water.
You who have no money, come!
Receive grain and eat;
come, without paying and without cost,
drink wine and milk! . . .
Heed me, and you shall eat well,
You shall delight in rich fare.
Come to me heedfully,
listen, that you may have life. (55, 1-3)

✿   ✿   ✿

The prophets had led the people of God from the Old Covenant to the New, from a collective religious experience to a personal one. They defined the conditions of this journey—trustful obedience, fidelity in love, faith capable of heroism, sincere desire of conversion, and total surrender from the bottom of the heart. Here their mission stops. Henceforth God's people lives in expectation. The Covenant of Sinai has run its course and the New Covenant is being born.

It would perhaps be more correct to say that that Israel has entered a period of trial. The promise of salvation is already operative, as though in advance, for those who are resolutely advancing towards the still invisible goal following the way indicated by the prophet. Goodwill, and the effort involved in the face of difficulties, will contribute in one way or another to arrive at the goal, and when they have done their best to understand his will, and follow it, God will judge that the time has come to accomplish the rest. Then the Word himself will become flesh, so that the word so often uttered and never perfectly understood may resound through the ages and in the hearts of many. Its eloquence will be irresistible not only because it is uttered by a human voice, but because it is proclaimed by the example of a whole lifetime beginning in Bethlehem and ending on Golgotha:

Thy will be done on earth as it is in heaven!
Thy will and not mine be done!

ISRAEL AND CHRISTIANITY

At the bidding of his God, Moses had planned the escape from Egypt of a band of serfs of his own race and had turned them into a people while leading them for half a lifetime through the desert. In the name of the same God, Joshua had led them to attack and conquer Canaan as a land of their own in which to live. Under David the work had been completed by the establishment of a kingdom unifying all the twelve tribes. The People of God settled down, became organized and prosperous, a small nation hemmed in by powerful empires like many others around her. She had found "a place in the sun" and, relying on a promise given to her by Yahveh, she expected to remain there indefinitely. The establishment of Israel in Palestine was a remarkable achievement, but it would have been even more remarkable if it had been permanent. It was contrary to geographical conditions and the laws of history.

Geographically, Israel's position in the western horn of the "fertile crescent" where it curves down towards Egypt made it an inevitable passage way, a kind of corridor, that any invading army was bound to take whatever direction it came from. Even supposing this small country had never found herself faced with the threat of direct aggression, she was always exposed to the danger of being trampled underfoot by armies heading for bigger prey; and besides the fact that her imprudent conduct was to turn the limelight on her, the particular structure of her territory as a natural fortress and an excellent base for launching operations offered too many advantages to the great powers for them to ignore her.

Historically as well, Israel could never hope to go on living in safety in her position between Egypt and the Mesopotamian empires, just as later she could not escape the armies of Alexander the Great and the eastward march of the Roman legions. It was impossible for such a tiny nation to maintain its independence against the irresistible power of warlike empires with limitless resources who aspired to world conquest.

Humanly speaking, Israel had had time to appear on the political chessboard only because of a fortunate combination of circumstances which had imposed a period of calm in the struggles between the great powers. The conquests of Thutmose III (c. 1503-1449 B.C.) had given Egypt an Asiatic empire to protect which she was obliged to interfere actively for a long period in the affairs of the countries to the north and east. The treaty between Ramses II and the Hittite empire seemed to be the prelude to a permanent peace, but it took only a few years for the situation to change. The Hittites disappeared for ever from the stage of history, and Egypt settled down to centuries of lethargy within her own borders. A free space was thus left between the Nile delta and the Euphrates at the very moment that the Israelites settled in Canaan in the conviction of remaining there for good.

A settlement which depended on the reawakening of the great empire could only be precarious. Two centuries after David the inevitable happened. Already in the previous century Israel had had an opportunity to foresee the danger when the armies of Salmanazar III had suddenly invaded Syria. This time the Assyrian forces were to submerge everything in their path on their victorious march into the Nile valley. The two small kingdoms which shared the heritage of David felt the wind of the hurricane passing over them and trembled for their own fate at seeing the disappearance of Damascus and the small principalities of northern Syria.

A few years later, after trying to ward off the danger by intrigues and alliances, Samaria fell in the unequal struggle. Judah, more fortunate, survived her for more than a century and a half. The breathing space afforded by the collapse of the Assyrian empire soon ended with the appearance of the equally aggressive Babylonians, and learning nothing from the example of Samaria, Jerusalem by her attempts to form military alliances drew down upon herself the same fate as her sister kingdom. The result was the captivity which to all appearances was to put a full stop to her history.

This small, obstinate, turbulent and foolhardy people continued to live on, however, amidst trials and repeated failures. In choosing them to serve His purpose, Yahveh had intended them for something different from the material prosperity of the kingdom of David where they could live in peace and be sheltered from the storms that raged about them. Though they were only dimly aware of its significance, God's choice of them was the preparation for the coming of another kingdom—the Kingdom which had been the object of the Promise—which would spread over the whole world and radically alter all its civilizations.

The geographical situation which prevented her from remaining shut up in herself served to further God's design. Palestine would be a crossroads through which mankind journeying in search of unity would be able to pass. Tossed about like a small boat on the waves, Israel would remain with her precious spiritual cargo intact; dispersion and all her other misfortunes would contribute to the spreading of her message.

So that His great design may be accomplished, the hand of Yahveh never ceases to guide and direct her in spite of her divisions and infidelities, rebellions and humiliations. It is for this that Israel continues to live, a contradiction and a paradox, nourishing dreams which are the more ambitious the more she is oppressed. But in order to keep alive, it is necessary for her to keep tight hold of the hand of her God. A first prophetic message lays on her the choice between life and death, between the destruction to which she would condemn herself by disregarding God's will and the difficult upward path in which he wishes to lead her. While Samaria is in her death throes Yahveh's voice is heard again in the rough imperative tones of Amos, and the gentler, sorrowful complaint of Hosea for a love betrayed. The prophet awakens in the heart of the prostituted people the memory of the freshness of the idyllic love that was born and flowered in the destitution of the desert. The unfaithful spouse has broken that marvelous union and all must be begun again from the beginning. Such is Yahveh's patience that he is ready even for this.

In the tragic hour when Jerusalem seemed destined to follow Samaria to her death and His design must be abandoned, Yahveh speaks a third time to his people through the mouth of Isaiah, the herald and champion of faith. Let Israel hearken to his message: Yahveh is present and his throne is nowhere but in Jerusalem. He fills the temple with the cloud of his smoke and the country with his glory. Though the nations rage against her, their tumult will be vain when they rush to the attack against Zion. No human agitation can alter the serenity or impair the majesty of Yahveh the King. Let Israel be submissive to her God and she will have nothing to fear, for her trial will end in triumph. That the trial will come there can be no doubt, for how can unclean man enter the world of purity where the thrice-holy God reigns? How can Israel pretend to remain sunk in ease and plenty when she must climb the rough path which leads to the summit where her God awaits her and she can only reach it by accepting the strictest purification? This is the price Yahveh demands for his intervention, and he will then draw down vengeance on his enemies and establish an ideal King over Israel to rule her with his spirit. He will not be simply a king like those whom Israel had known from David onwards. When faith has been cleansed by trial, this king will arise and his reign will have no comparison with anything ever known. At this point the messianic message of the Bible is fully asserted. Israel has taken a road which, not less than other peoples, she herself could never have imagined. She is withdrawn from the fluctuations of history and settled unshaken on a Rock dominating events. Her task is to bring about the realization of the mystery of God's purpose.

The absolute originality of Israel's destiny is shown a century later in the most paradoxical manner. Before she can meet with triumph she must submit not only to a heavy trial, but to death itself. She must die to rise purer, stronger, lovelier. She must die, but not like the small states around her with their national gods who are swept away by the powers of the world. Her destiny is not on a par with theirs. Israel will live again in a different way. Jeremiah announces the immutable decree of Yahveh: the kingdom of Israel is condemned and its temple will be destroyed. The condemnation and the destruction must not be attributed to material forces, which are only the intruments, but to Israel's sin in rejecting the hand of God. Yahveh would never be content with partial submission; what he asks for is the whole and entire being. But man is incapable of submitting completely to God; he has shown only too clearly that there is nothing but resistance and disloyalty in him. The old Israel must die so that Yahveh can create a new Israel with a submissive and faithful heart.

Henceforth the religion of Israel will be a religion of the heart. There will be no more need, at least for a time, of the outward structures in which her life was organized. The true worship that God requires can do without the Temple, the Holy

City and the throne of David, because it will be interior and personal, and every man will be personally responsible to God for his faith.

The new Israel according to God's heart will be formed on the banks of the Euphrates. To Ezekiel is given the hard task of persuading his fellow-exiles that salvation is in their own hands and that they must not look back nostalgically to a past which has been condemned because it was sinful. Israel is under sentence of death, but whoever refuses to accept this necessary death will have no share in the resurrection. When Jerusalem finally falls under the hammer blows of the Babylonians despite a desperate resistance, Ezekiel is free to call up the image of an ideal Israel cleansed from the sin of the gentiles and from all impurity. His vision was doubtless a utopian one, but it cannot be called vain, for it was the vision that was to nourish the hearts of the Jews after the Exile and enable them to prepare themselves for the entry into the Kingdom of God.

When, after Babylon in her turn disappears from the scene, the Israelites are delivered from captivity and joyfully traverse the desert to return home, they may begin to hope that the time has at last come for the final Kingdom of Yahveh. The Second Isaiah believes it so, but though his vision of a new world is still afar off, his burning message serves as a preparation for the acceptance of the Resurrection mystery. A Voice rises above a passing world to summon to life, the same Voice that once summoned the whole of creation into existence. The great prophets sink into silence at this triumphal cry. So long the messengers of death, they are now the heralds of final salvation.

Such was the strange and wonderful road God set before the people whom he had chosen. Alone among all the nations who have peopled the earth, Israel advanced along it to obtain for them a deliverance and a means of self-development they could not even imagine, and which she herself only vaguely glimpsed. Along it she was guided and sustained by the ungentle but firm and loving hand that resolutely snatched her from death to draw her to life which to give in abundance he asked nothing from her but a trustful renunciation such as that which a broken but serene voice was to murmur from the height of the Cross:

Into Thy hands I commend my spirit.

CHRONOLOGICAL TABLE

Kings of Israel		Kings of Judah		Kings of Assyria	
931-913	Jeroboam	931-910	Rehoboam		
783-743	Jeroboam II	781-740	Azariah		
743	Zechariah				
743	Shallum	740-736	Jotham	740-728	Tiglath-Pileser III
743-738	Menahem	736-716	Ahaz	727-722	Salmanasar V
738-737	Pekahiah	721	Fall of Samaria	721-705	Sargon II
737-732	Pekah				
732-724	Hoshea				

Kings of Judah		Kings of Assyria		Kings of Babylon	
736-716	Ahaz	721-705	Sargon II		
716-687	Hezekiah	705-681	Sennacherib		
687-642	Manasseh	680-669	Assurhaddon		
642-640	Amon	669-626	Assurbanipal	626-605	Nabopolassar
640-609	Josiah	612	Fall of Nineveh	605-562	Nebuchadnezzar
609-598	Jehoiakim				
598	Jehoiachin				
598-587	Zedekiah				

Fall of Jerusalem: July 587
Cyrus the Great, king of the Persians: 557-529